The 101 Sexiest, Craziest, Most Outrageous Agony Column Questions (And Answers) Of All Time

What the papers say about Dr Vernon Coleman and his books

- 'Vernon Coleman writes brilliant books' The Good Book Guide
- 'The revered guru of medicine' Nursing Times
- 'Perhaps the best known health writer in the world today.' The Therapist
- 'The Lone Ranger, Robin Hood and the Equalizer rolled into one.' Evening Times
- 'Britain's leading health care campaigner' The Sun
- 'Britain's leading medical author' The Daily Star
- 'Brilliant' The People
- 'The patient's champion' Birmingham Post
- 'The medical expert you can't ignore' Sunday Independent
- 'Dr Coleman writes with more sense than bias' Daily Express
- 'Outspoken and alert observer' Sunday Express
- 'All commonsense and no nonsense' Health Services Management
- 'Vernon Coleman is the people's doctor' Devon Life
- 'The doctor who dares to speak his mind' Oxford Mail
- 'Refreshingly sensible' Spectator
- 'He writes lucidly and wittily' Good Housekeeping
- 'The doctor with the common touch' Birmingham Post
- 'Clear and helpful' The Guardian
- 'His message is important' The Economist
- 'It's impossible not to be impressed' Western Daily Press
- 'Refreshingly forthright' Liverpool Daily Post

What a few of Dr Coleman's readers have to say:

- 'Your willingness to say exactly what you think is a refreshing change.' P.H., Hants

- 'I admire your forthright and refreshingly honest way of expressing your views and opinions...bless you for being a light in the eternal darkness.' B.O., Durham

- 'If only more people in the medical profession and this government were like you it would be a much nicer world.' G.W., Hants

- 'My deep appreciation for your great courage and integrity over the years.' J.T., U.S.A.

- 'I have never before had the patience to sit down and read a book but once I started your book a few weeks ago I was riveted.' S.R., Birmingham

- 'I admire your direct approach and philosophy in respect of general health.' A.W., Durham

- 'It's lovely to have someone who cares about people as you do. You tell us such a lot of things that we are afraid to ask our own doctors.' K.C., Newcastle

- 'I would like to thank you for telling us the truth' R.K., Kent

- 'I feel I must write and congratulate you ... your no-nonsense attitude, teamed with plain common sense makes a refreshing change...Please keep up the good work' L.B., Leics

- 'Thanks over and over again – good health always to you as you are fighting for a good cause in life – for the sick' E.H., Cleveland

- 'I only wish to God that we had a few such as your good self in parliament, then maybe our standard of life would possibly be better' H.H., Somerset

- 'I greatly admire your no nonsense approach to things and your acting as champion of the people' L.A., Cornwall

- 'I have now read and studied all your excellent books and have enjoyed and benefited from them immensely' B.B., Dorset

- 'Your no nonsense approach to the medical profession is a tonic' C.S., Tyne & Wear

- 'I admire your courage to speak out for what you believe to be the truth' E.C., Northants

- 'May I say that I think you have done a real service to all those who have the sense and patience to study your books' B.A., Hampshire

- 'I've just read *Bodypower* and *Food for Thought*. They will now go onto my bookshelf to be re-read many times in the future.' G.G., Bucks

BOOKS BY VERNON COLEMAN

The Medicine Men (1975)
Paper Doctors (1976)
Everything You Want To Know About Ageing (1976)
Stress Control (1978)
The Home Pharmacy (1980)
Aspirin or Ambulance (1980)
Face Values (1981)
Guilt (1982)
The Good Medicine Guide (1982)
Stress And Your Stomach (1983)
Bodypower (1983)
An A to Z Of Women's Problems (1984)
Bodysense (1984)
Taking Care Of Your Skin (1984)
Life Without Tranquillisers (1985)
High Blood Pressure (1985)
Diabetes (1985)
Arthritis (1985)
Eczema and Dermatitis (1985)
The Story Of Medicine (1985, 1998)
Natural Pain Control (1986)
Mindpower (1986)
Addicts and Addictions (1986)
Dr Vernon Coleman's Guide To Alternative Medicine (1988)
Stress Management Techniques (1988)
Overcoming Stress (1988)
Know Yourself (1988)
The Health Scandal (1988)
The 20 Minute Health Check (1989)
Sex For Everyone (1989)
Mind Over Body (1989)
Eat Green Lose Weight (1990)
Toxic Stress (1991)
Why Animal Experiments Must Stop (1991)

The Drugs Myth (1992)
Why Doctors Do More Harm Than Good (1993)
Stress and Relaxation (1993)
Complete Guide to Sex (1993)
How to Conquer Backache (1993)
How to Conquer Arthritis (1993)
Betrayal of Trust (1994)
Know Your Drugs (1994, 1997)
Food for Thought (1994)
The Traditional Home Doctor (1994)
I Hope Your Penis Shrivels Up (1994)
People Watching (1995)
Relief from Irritable Bowel Syndrome (1995)
The Parent's Handbook (1995)
Oral Sex: Bad Taste And Hard To Swallow? (1995)
Why Is Pubic Hair Curly? (1995)
Men in Dresses (1996)
Power over Cancer (1996)
Crossdressing (1996)
How To Get The Best Out Of Prescription Drugs (1996)
How To Get The Best Out of Alternative Medicine (1996)
How To Conquer Arthritis (1996)
High Blood Pressure (1996)
How To Stop Your Doctor Killing You (1996)
How To Overcome Toxic Stress (1996)
Fighting For Animals (1996)
Alice and Other Friends (1996)
Dr Vernon Coleman's Fast Action Health Secrets (1997)
Dr Vernon Coleman's Guide to Vitamins and Minerals (1997)
Spiritpower (1997)
Other People's Problems (1998)
How To Publish Your Own Book (1999)
How To Relax and Overcome Stress (1999)
Animal Rights – Human Wrongs (1999)

novels
The Village Cricket Tour (1990)
The Bilbury Chronicles (1992)
Bilbury Grange (1993)
Mrs Caldicot's Cabbage War (1993)
The Man Who Inherited a Golf Course (1993)
Bilbury Revels (1994)
Deadline (1994)
Bilbury Country (1996)
Second Innings (1999)

short stories
Bilbury Pie (1995)

on cricket
Thomas Winsden's Cricketing Almanack (1983)
Diary Of A Cricket Lover (1984)

as Edward Vernon
Practice Makes Perfect (1977)
Practise What You Preach (1978)
Getting Into Practice (1979)
Aphrodisiacs – An Owner's Manual (1983)
Aphrodisiacs – An Owner's Manual (Turbo Edition) (1984)
The Complete Guide To Life (1984)

as Marc Charbonnier
Tunnel (novel 1980)

with Dr Alan C Turin
No More Headaches (1981)

with Alice
Alice's Diary (1989)
Alice's Adventures (1992)

The 101 Sexiest, Craziest, Most Outrageous Agony Column Questions (And Answers) Of All Time

Vernon Coleman

Edited by

Donna Antoinette Davidson

Blue Books

Published by Blue Books, Publishing House, Trinity Place, Barnstaple, Devon EX32 9HJ, England.

Note: This book contains questions and answers which appeared in the author's column in The Sunday People newspaper.

ISBN: 1899726 11 X

A catalogue record for this book is available from the British Library.

Printed by J.W Arrowsmith Ltd., Bristol

Dirty Post

My boyfriend is working away from home. He has asked me to post him personal items from my dirty laundry. In particular he wants me to send him my knickers and bras. I don't particularly mind sending him these things but I can't imagine what he wants them for. My first thought was that he might be a secret transvestite but he is much bigger than I am and I don't think he would fit into any of my underwear.

I don't think your boyfriend wants to wear your dirty underwear. (If he was a transvestite he wouldn't have stipulated that it be dirty). I have tried (in vain) to think of ways to be tasteful about this. Close your eyes everyone else. I think your boy friend wants your underwear to help provide him with a little physical stimulation and sensory enhancement during solitary, manual sexual adventures. Are you with me? No? Oh dear. Can't you please find someone else to explain it to you? The rest of you can open your eyes again now, by the way.

••

Vibrator Addict

I am addicted to my vibrator. I used to masturbate with my fingers but after I discovered the vibrator I abandoned this method. My boyfriend says that regular use of the vibrator may damage my reproductive organs and that I should stop using it. Is there any truth in this?

It depends entirely on what you do with it. If you use the vibrator to stimulate your clitoris then your reproductive organs are unlikely to be affected. Maybe your boyfriend is simply jealous of the fact that a piece of plastic with a battery in it has given already given you more orgasms than he could hope to give you in a lifetime of enthusiastic love making. And maybe you should listen to him. Your vibrator may be efficient but it won't be much good when you want a cuddle.

●●

In Love With My Dentist's Nurse

I am in love with my dentist's nurse. I love the way her breasts press against my arm when she's holding the little sucker thing in my mouth. She uses a perfume which drives me wild. I keep eating lots of sweets so that my teeth will need lots of attention. Do you think all the sugar will have any other bad effects on my health?

You will become so grotesquely obese that you will not fit into the dentist's chair. And will she find you irresistible when all your teeth have fallen out and you have only a pair of gums to offer her? You will save your health, your teeth and your pocket considerable pain by asking the nurse if she wants to go out with you. But please be warned: the fact that a nurse accidentally presses her breasts against your arm when she is holding a sucker in your mouth doesn't mean that she wants to rush home with you and play 'let's tickle my fancy' and 'where shall we hide the folding umbrella'.

●●

Not Particularly Well Endowed

My boyfriend isn't particularly well endowed. In fact, he has the smallest wotsit I've ever come across. Do you remember those men who do a balloon dance when in

the nude – hiding their vital parts behind balloons?
Well, my boyfriend can hide his wotsit behind a balloon
without blowing it up. I love him very much and we have
great fun together but I find sex with him frustrating and
rather unsatisfying. I would be grateful for any advice
you can give me.

Sorry to hear you drew a short straw in the great winkle-picking lottery. You'll get more satisfaction if you choose the right positions. Incidentally, it causes me great distress to hear such a proud and vital organ described yet again as a 'wotsit'. It makes it sound like something you pick up by the dozen in a blister pack at the local ironmongers. If you find yourself unable to use the word 'penis' without coming out in a rash of rosy embarrassment then I suggest that the word 'gladius' would make a good alternative. Gladius is the Latin word for 'sword', and seems particularly appropriate since the word 'vagina' is the Latin for sheath or scabbard. The average roman soldier was always slipping his gladius into a handy vagina. Since most of us like to create nicknames – often shortened versions of existing names – for those whom we love, the term 'glad' would, I suggest, be a suitable term of endearment for the penis. The phrase 'I'm feeling glad all over' would then take on an entirely new meaning. (I wonder how many of the posh, unmanageable and boring papers provide their readers with Latin lessons on a Sunday?)

•••

Flat, Limp And Very Warm

When I make sandwiches for my boyfriend he likes me
to sit on them for 30 minutes before he arrives home.
When he eats them they are rather flat, limp and very
warm but he says that they are the best he has ever
eaten. We have wonderful sex afterwards. Do you know
if anyone else ever does this? Is it a fetish and if so is
there a name for it?

The name for the fetish you describe is buttybumflattenphilia and it was first described by Professor Otto Gherkin in a special supplement to the European Medical Journal in 1978. I am told that this fetish is now so popular that large scale purveyors of take away snacks employ thousands of women to do nothing other than sit down on sandwiches. A large bottom is apparently considered to be a great asset in this particular area of catering. Some women can flatten three sandwiches or two crusty rolls at a time. Large scale sellers of sandwiches have tried introducing mechanical aids but there is apparently no substitute for a female bottom when it comes to properly compressing a sandwich and giving it that 'je ne sais quoi'. A spokesman for one large chain of stores told me that tuna is the most popular bumpressed sandwich they do. If you want to try one just ask for the 'gluteal-special'. The buttybumflattenphilia fetish is common throughout North America and in many Northern Europe countries but is not widely known in Scandinavia where the popularity of the open sandwich makes it something of a non starter.

●●

The Woman Next Door

I am a 19 year old male student living in a bedsit. The window of my room looks straight into the lounge of the house next door. The house is occupied by a couple in their forties. My desk, where I work most evenings, is right next to the window. For some time now, at about half past four, the woman next door has walked into their lounge wearing either a see through shortie nightie or suspenders, stockings and a tiny bra. She is very attractive and has a terrific figure. She waters the plants on her window sill and then sits down and watches television. Occasionally she eats a banana – very suggestively. Every so often she looks directly at my window and smiles at me. Once she waved. At about 7.00 pm she disappears and gets dressed. Her husband arrives home at about 7.30 pm and usually draws the curtains. Sometimes, when her husband has gone to bed, she will come down in a nightie, draw the curtains back, put on the lights and stand there for a while. She is obviously aware that I can see her. Do you think she is just an exhibitionist or do you think she wants me to go round to her house?

You could get a pretty good idea of exactly what is on offer by popping round to see your neighbour one afternoon at about 4.30 pm. Use your imagination. Tell her your pencil is blunt and ask if she has anything you can use to put a better end on it. If she invites you in then you are on your own I'm afraid. But before you make this move do please be sure you want more than a free floorshow from your neighbour. Don't go knocking on doors if you aren't prepared for them to be opened. If your curvaceous neighbour welcomes you with open arms and legs are you going to accept what is on offer – together with the attendant risks?

●●●

A Computer Freak

My boyfriend is a computer freak. He works with computers and spends much of his free time with his computer. I recently found him sitting in front of his computer masturbating. He confessed that he was having what he called 'cybersex' with a woman called Dolly who lives in California. He told me that he regularly had 'cybersex' both with this blonde called Dolly (who apparently has a 44 DD chest) and with quite a number of other women. He says that it wasn't being unfaithful and that he didn't see why he should stop.

I don't think you need worry too much about 'Dolly'. 'She' is probably male, in his early twenties, overweight, a burger addict and the proud owner of an olive green anorak – in other words a real nerd. Most cybersex affairs consist of two sad nerds, separated by many miles of telephone cable, eagerly tossing themselves off into paper tissues. It's the only way the average computer freak can turn software into hardware and then back again into software. If this is the twentieth century computer freak's idea of great romance then the word 'sad' is probably the most appropriate description I can think of. Try asking your boyfriend what is missing from your relationship – and what he is trying to replace by these sorry masturbatory adventures. Does he want more sex or more excitement? Can you re-boot your relationship? If he refuses to talk or tell you what he wants from you (and life) then perhaps you should simply pull the plug on him and leave him to tip toe fruitlessly through his ethereal fantasy world.

••

Office Party

At Christmas I went to an office party. I wore a tight fitting mini skirt without any knickers and I put on a semi see through blouse. I never wear a bra even though I have quite full breasts. The only underwear I wore was a suspender belt and a pair of black, seamed stockings. Just as I was about to leave the house my boyfriend grabbed me, said I made him feel randy, and had sex with me. At the end of the evening three male friends offered to take me home from the office. One drove, one sat in the front and the third got into the back of the car with me. He immediately started fondling me and kissing my breasts through my blouse. He then quickly unfastened my blouse and pulled my skirt down. Within minutes I found myself being made love to, virtually naked, as we drove along. The guy who was making love to me seemed to come for ever. When he had finished the driver stopped the car, two of the guys swapped places and the man who had been in the front passenger seat made love to me. Eventually, all three of them made love to me. When they finally dropped me back at the flat my boyfriend wanted to make love again. I was a complete mess and I thought he'd guess what must have happened but he didn't. I'm now worried that I might get pregnant. Is it possible that the amount of come that was spurted into me could have overcome the protection of the contraceptive pill which I take? It is one of the ordinary oestrogen-progestogen 'combined' pills.

The pill you take works by preventing ovulation so the amount of sperm deposited inside you has no effect on your chances of becoming pregnant. The sperm swimming around are going to be constantly disappointed without any eggs to fertilize. But it would be sensible for you to check that your busy evening has not left you with any infection.

●●●

Exceedingly Frustrating

When my husband makes love to me he can only manage a maximum of 64 ins and outs before he comes. Sometimes he manages as few as 16. The count for the last three times we have made love has been 20,26 and 22. I find this exceedingly frustrating because I estimate that I would need at least 120 ins and outs to reach a climax.

I assume that you are using the phrase 'in and out' to describe a complete cycle of intravaginal penile movement and my sympathies lie entirely with your husband. The prospect of making love to a sexual accounts clerk who keeps a record of every oscillation is enough to make the firmest member of the human race wilt and shrivel. Making love to you sounds as though it would be about as much fun as listening to a party political broadcast. Most women fail to orgasm during sex but find other ways to achieve satisfaction and I suggest that next time you and your husband end up in bed together you leave your calculator on the landing and concentrate instead on enjoying yourself. Offering your unfortunate and long suffering spouse some encouragement and praise would be a sound first move.

●●

My Boyfriend Has A Large One

My boyfriend has a very large one, if you know what I mean. So far, although I've played around with it quite a lot I haven't actually let him put it inside me. But the problem is that I promised to let him give me one for Christmas. It seemed a good idea at the time because I'm broke and I couldn't afford an adjustable wrench which is the other thing I know he wants. But I'm now beginning to get cold feet. The thing is that his penis is much bigger than anything I've ever had in me before. Even when limp it is bigger than my last boyfriend's was when erect. Do you think I'll be able to cope? Do you have any tips?

I feel sure that you will be able to cope just as long as you relax properly. A vagina can stretch wide enough to accommodate a baby's head so, unless your boyfriend's penis is thicker and more solid than a baby's head, you should be able to cope perfectly well. (If your boyfriend's penis is thicker and more solid than a baby's head do please get in touch because Trixie, Jakki, Loosie, Fyona, Dafne and several of my other personal assistants would like to meet him in order to conduct experimental research of a purely scientific nature.)

●●

Two Girls And A Dildo

I'm 22 and recently changed jobs and moved to London where I now rent a room in a flat. The other two occupants of the flat, Jane and Karen, are girls in their mid twenties. They share the only other bedroom. My girlfriend was initially a little dubious about my sharing with two women but eventually accepted that the arrangement was purely one of convenience. I haven't had much to do with either of the girls because I often work late in the evenings and most weekends I go back up north to be with my girlfriend, but last Wednesday when the trains were on strike I accepted a lift from my boss and arrived back at the flat much earlier than I usually do. I walked into the living room and had the shock of my life when I saw Jane and Karen, who were both entirely naked, sprawled on the sofa watching a porno movie. They didn't seem in the slightest bit embarrassed. There was a dildo lying on the sofa between them. Jane offered me a glass of wine and neither of them made any attempt to cover up. It turned out that the two girls are lesbians and that although they have a rather 'loose' and uncommitted relationship they have been sleeping and living together for four years. Jane told me that she was bisexual but Karen admitted that her only sexual experience with a man had been such a disaster that she was really still a virgin. After we'd opened another bottle of wine Jane suggested to Karen that she ought to take advantage of the situation to find out what sex with a man – meaning me – was really like. At first I thought she was joking but realised she wasn't when she reached over, unfastened my trousers, took out my penis and started playing with it. I ended up making love to both of them and had the most amazing evening of my life. Afterwards we even slept together in their bed.

To my amazement the two girls seem to regard the evening as of no great significance. The following evening I asked Karen if she'd like to go out for a meal but she said that she was still a lesbian and not inter-ested in a heterosexual relationship. I feel as though I've been used. I don't know whether to stay in the flat or move out and I don't know whether to tell my girl-friend or whether to keep quiet.

You will have to get used to the fact that after being used as a living, breathing dildo you have been discarded like an old con-dom (I hope you used condoms, by the way. If you didn't then do pop along to your local Furtive Look Clinic and have your twiddly bits peeped at by experts in white coats who know about these things. Lesbians aren't immune to sexually transmitted diseases). I don't think you should tell your girlfriend about your unsuccessful attempt to convert the natives. A confession might help you unload some of your guilt but it won't improve her life. If you can lock the memory of your orgiastic evening away in a little compartment under the heading 'Isolated Erotic Incidents' then stay in the flat. If you think you'll find that difficult to do then you should start looking for ac-commodation elsewhere.

• •

Is This Harmful?

Is it harmful to swallow semen? I enjoy swallowing my own semen after I have ejaculated.

You are unlikely to give yourself any infection that you have not already got and can, therefore, continue with your feasting with relative impunity. Semen is low-fat, low-sodium, caffeine-free, and contains no sugar or preservatives. The International Semen Institute, of which I am proud to be patron, recommends a maximum daily intake of 10 mls.

●●

Telephone Sex

My boyfriend is a salesman and has to spend a lot of time away from home. A few months ago we both saw a film in which the two lead characters talked dirty to each other on the telephone. We now do this regularly two or three times a week and both find it a very satisfying way to get rid of our sexual frustrations. Do you think it can do any harm?

No. You won't go blind or even short sighted. And you won't grow hair on the palms of your hands. But I do have one warning for you. Make sure that it's your boyfriend on the phone before you go into your telephone routine. A friend of mine (whose husband was working away from home) used to have telephone sex every Wednesday at 10.00 pm. One evening the phone went as usual and she picked it up and went straight into action. 'I'm wearing my sexy black undies,' she began breathlessly. 'I'm taking my bra off and fondling my breasts. What are you doing?' 'I was ringing to tell you that my husband would be round tomorrow to repair your central heating boiler,' said a rather cold, feminine voice. 'But it doesn't sound to me as though you need any central heating and even if you do it certainly won't be my husband coming to repair your boiler.' My friend says that this was terrible for three reasons. First, she had been waiting two weeks for the boiler to be repaired. Second, when her husband did ring she was in such a state that she was is no condition to talk sexy. And third, she later discovered that the boiler repairer's son was in the same class as her own at the local school. 'I could never look that woman in the face,' she told me. 'And I was terribly relieved when they left the area.'

●●

My Son's Friend

I am a 37 year old divorced woman with an 18 year old son who has just started college. Last weekend my son came home for the first time and brought a friend with him. On Sunday morning I had to go into the room in which my son's friend was staying to get something out of a cupboard. I knocked on the door, went in, got what I wanted and then looked round to see that my son's friend had pushed back the bed clothes and was lying there quite naked with a very noticeable erection. I blushed when I saw it because it has been several years since I saw a man in that state. He then asked me to fondle him. I didn't really want to but I'm afraid I couldn't help myself. I put down the things I'd collected and sat on the edge of the bed. I then played with my son's friend until he came while he fondled my breasts through my jumper. When I left the bedroom I was so aroused that I had to lock myself in my room for a while. I'm sure you can imagine why. Neither of us said anything about it afterwards but when he left my son's friend thanked me and said he hoped I'd let him come to stay again. My son has rung twice since but he hasn't mentioned his friend and I haven't mentioned him either, of course. However, I find myself thinking about him all the time and if he does come back to stay I just know I will find an excuse to go into his room again. I really don't know what to do. Part of me wants to try and get in touch with the boy to see if we can develop some sort of relationship, after all the age difference isn't all that great. Part of me says this is crazy and I should just forget all about him. What do you think I should do?

I hate to be brutal but I'm afraid I think you should try to forget about him. It doesn't sound to me as if your son's friend really wanted a proper relationship so much as a quick thrill. And think about your son. If you start an affair with his chum what is that going to do to your relationship with him? Age need not be a barrier to love but, sadly, I don't really think this sounds like a romance made in heaven.

• •

Suck, Blow And Nibble

My girlfriend wants me to perform oral sex on her but I'm not sure what to do. I asked a friend and he said I should just suck and blow and nibble her with my teeth.

If you believe all that you are a sucker. Never blow – it can be dangerous. Keep your teeth well out of the way – preferably in a glass on the bedside table – and concentrate on using your tongue. Exercise your tongue by licking the last bit of ice cream out of a tall sundae glass and using it to tie reef knots in pieces of dental floss.

• •

Penis For Sale

I was interested to read that surgeons find it difficult to provide proper genitals for women wanting to become functional men. If surgeons write to me I will be willing to sell my penis (seven inches long when erect) and testicles for £1,000,000. I have fathered healthy children but am willing to call it a day on the subject of coition for recreation or procreation. I would like to buy a Rolls Royce motor car since our Ford is now over ten years old and is beginning to give us troubles mechanically. I had to have the ignition switch replaced recently and was warned that the cam belt will soon need replacing at a considerable cost. I would also like to have a reliable urine disposal arrangement. If a buyer is found ready and able to meet the terms of my offer I will give you exclusive photos. NB I have not discussed the above with my wife yet so be prepared to cancel the offer if she objects.

I really do think you ought to speak to your wife before you continue with your plan to start flogging off the family jewels. I have no doubt that a surgeon could transplant your penis and testicles onto a woman keen to acquire male physical characteristics but fear that the price you are asking might prove to be rather a stumbling block – particularly when you remember that fees for surgeons, lawyers and surveyors would have to be added on top of your million. Transsexuals are not particularly common and I would imagine that millionaire transsexuals are about as thin on the ground as thoughtful, sensitive politicians. I can't see many bank managers being eager to offer mortgage facilities to would be purchasers of your reproductive equipment, in fine condition (one careful owner) though it might be.

●●

Willing Sex Slave

I have become my boss's willing sex slave. Two months ago I made a mistake while typing an important contract and as a result my boss lost a lot of money. Instead of firing me he told me to take down my tights and knickers and lie across his lap so that he could smack my bottom. I allowed him to do this because I desperately wanted to keep my job and I realised that I deserved to be punished. He did not smack me very hard and afterwards I found myself fantasising about the experience. When I deliberately made another mistake two days later I told him that he could smack my bottom again if he wanted. This time I had worn a very tight dress so that I had to strip completely for the smacking. I also wore stockings and a suspender belt instead of tights. After he had smacked my bottom I could see that he was very aroused. I played with him and then we made love on his desk. After this had happened five times my boss guessed that I was making mistakes on purpose. He told me that he was worried that all my mistakes might put him out of business so we agreed that he would punish me every evening whether I had made any mistakes or not. I am now his complete sex slave. We have a normal working relationship during office hours but every evening at five o'clock I let him have his way with me. Every day I am constantly moist with excitement and anticipation. He smacks my bottom half a dozen times with his bare hand and then I let him do what he wants. Do you think I am kinky?

An academic study conducted by three ditch diggers and a crane driver recently showed that every evening, in offices everywhere, typists, secretaries and personal assistants bare their bottoms and bend over to atone for the day's misdeeds. Walk along the corridors of any large office building and you will hear the gentle slap of palm on buttock coming from behind 28% of all closed doors. In council office buildings you will hear this sound behind 77% of closed doors, though in 36% of cases it is the secretary who is doing the smacking and the boss who is bent over with his trousers down around his ankles. It is acknowledged by the European Union that deliberate mistakes made by secretaries and bosses wanting to get their bottoms smacked are responsible for a vast amount of lost business every year.

•••

Crazy About Me

I have two girlfriends who are both crazy about me. One is a very good looking blonde and our friends all say that we make a really terrific looking couple. The snag with her is that she's a bit thick. The other one isn't all that much to look at but she's devoted to me and will do anything I tell her to do. She's quite a good cook and I think she would make a good housewife. My boss has told me that I won't get promotion at work until I'm married. I'm very tempted to marry the good looking girl (who is slightly the best in bed) but something tells me that maybe the other girl might, in the long run, make a better overall bet. I talked it over with a mate and he said that I should marry the one who would be good around the house because a good pair of legs don't last for ever. I don't want to make a mistake. What do you think I should do?

First, I would like to thank you for writing to me.

Since you have honoured me by asking for my advice I'm tempted to tell you that you should get a large pan, fill it with water, put it on the stove and then put your head in it. (Incidentally, you must have a very large head to contain all that conceit so it would obviously need to be a very large pan). Or that you should fill a bath with petrol, sit in it and play with matches. Or that you should take up parachute jumping and get someone with uncontrollable homicidal tendencies to pack your parachute.

But I won't tell you to do any of these things because you are such a moron that you would probably do them and then there would be an inquest and I'd have to go and that would be boring.

I would suggest that you buy a plastic blow up doll and marry that but even plastic blow up dolls must have some standards, expectations and rights.

So I suggest that you give up your job and both girlfriends and take up masturbation as a full time career.

You are, after all, already a complete wanker.

● ●

Party Trick

Two weeks ago while we were fooling around in a hotel bedroom my husband picked up my handbag and hung it on his erect penis. Since then he's done this several times and it has become a sort of 'party trick'. He keeps putting more and more things into the bag and is now threatening to do it next time we have visitors. I'm worried that he may damage himself permanently because presumably the penis isn't built for carrying around heavy weights.

The load bearing capacity of the erect human penis is around 5 to 6 pounds but this is generally regarded as a theoretical capacity rather than a practical capability.

It is not unusual for the penis to be used as a stage prop for circus tricks. For example, hoopla is regarded as an entertaining alternative in some areas and participants use old bicycle tyres, doughnuts or polo mints depending upon the circumference of the target.

I strongly advise against any such activity. The erect penis is a delicate and sensitive piece of equipment which should be treated with care and respect at all times.

● ●

Turned On By Gay Men (And I'm A Woman)

I am a married woman. I am really turned on by gay men. I find the thought of men kissing, fondling and having sex extremely erotic. I love watching films with even a vague homosexual content. My husband thinks I am weird. Do you think I have a problem?

No. An entirely unreliable survey of female shop assistants showed that 57% were turned on by the thought of men kissing one another. Since far more reliable surveys have shown that 99.99% of men are turned on by watching (or thinking about) women having lesbian sex this research simply confirms that what is good for the gander is just as good for the goose.

●●●

I Treat Him Like A Slave

A few months ago I asked my boyfriend to move out of my flat. He was very upset and pleaded with me to let him stay. I agreed on condition that he abided by my rules. Since then he has carried out all the housework and I treat him like a slave. I often make him dress in women's clothes.

He looks very fetching in a French Maid's uniform when doing the hoovering and the polishing. At first he was reluctant but the new relationship has brought out his submissive nature, just as it has brought out my hitherto dormant dominant nature. I still love him, but in a different way.

Occasionally, as a special reward I let him have sex but usually I just make him masturbate as this really turns me on. I make him perform oral on me whenever I demand. After being with a fairly boring and selfish partner I now enjoy the attentions of a dedicated, hard working, anxious to please servant.

It is often said that for a relationship to succeed there must be some give and take. You and your partner seem to have discovered a variation on the perfect relationship: he gives and you take.

Since you both seem to be happy with this balance I can see no reason why you should not continue to enjoy one another in this relatively unusual way for many years to come. (I have a powerful feeling that approximately 76% of the population will read your letter with a certain amount of envy.)

• •

Two Brothers In A Bar

While on a camping holiday with a friend I met two really nice brothers in a bar. They asked us to go dancing. After we had agreed to go out with them my girlfriend chickened out. She has a boyfriend and said she didn't want to be unfaithful to him.

I went with them on my own and we had a lot of good laughs. Afterwards I went back to their tent for a drink. While we were fooling around one of them bet me that the three of us could all get into the same sleeping bag. I could see what was coming so I refused but they both bet me that they wouldn't get erections and that therefore nothing would happen. So, for a laugh, I said I'd do it. We had to take all our clothes off to get into the sleeping bag but as soon as we were in both of them got erections and the sleeping bag got even more crowded. One of them pointed out that we'd all be a lot more comfortable if I let them do the obvious with their erections. They both bet me that they wouldn't come. Well, they both lost that bet as well! Twice each! When I got up to go back to my tent the next morning another holiday-maker saw them giving me the money I had won and started a nasty rumour around the camp that I was 'on the game'. The two boys confirmed that my account of what had happened was true but when my friend heard the rumour she made me give her half of the money. She now says that if I don't give her the rest she will tell my boyfriend what happened.

31

Foreign Objects

Isn't life a bitch? I think you are very, very unlucky to have such a distrusting friend. I can't imagine how she can possibly be so suspicious. You are obviously a very nice and innocent girl. Never mind. To cheer you up I'll send you a shoe box full of used notes if you can send me incontrovertible evidence proving that your story is true. I'll also have my ears pierced, paint all my nails bright pink and wear a frock for a week. I'll have your name tattooed at the top of my left leg and I'll let you pull the other one (the one that has got bells on it) as much as you like. What more can I say?

••

Foreign Objects

My husband is constantly begging me to let him put a variety of objects inside me – bananas, cucumbers, candles, roll on deodorant stick. If I refuse we argue and he sulks. I wouldn't mind if he wanted to do these things as part of love making – but to him I'm just a sex object. He took topless photos of me and although he promised not to show anyone he had shown them to a friend within two days. He made a video of us making love and took the tape round to show his friend. I would love to leave him but I have nowhere to go.

Sex games have to be fun and both partners have to be willing. Otherwise they aren't games. Your husband is simply using and abusing you and he sounds about as much fun as herpes. Encourage your husband to keep doing the shopping by telling him that he hasn't yet brought home anything to which you really fancy making love. Soon your house will be stocked entirely with phallic shaped groceries and toiletries. But you will have been able to save the housekeeping money. And within six months you should be able to tell the pathetic old fool the location of another secret burial place for his collection of fruit, vegetables and roll on deodorants.

••

Single Stripper

I am a single mother and I supplement my income by
stripping in a pub on Sunday lunchtimes. Last Saturday
evening my boyfriend made love to me on the carpet in
my living room. When I went to work the following day
one of the other girls pointed out that I had 'carpet
burns' all over my back and bum. I had to do my whole
act without turning round. The pub landlord wasn't very
pleased because quite a few of his customers like
seeing the girls' bottoms. Can you give me some advice
for the future please?

This has got to be the oddest letter I've had since the one I
received from a reader who wanted to know where she could
buy something called dolly blue. In future I suggest that you enjoy
your Saturday evening nookie on your knees. I doubt if any discern-
ing member of a strip show audience would notice your knees if you
painted them bright green with yellow spots on so carpet burns will
go quite unnoticed.

●●●

Blushes

I blush a lot and I wish I didn't. What is worse I often
blush because I have thought of something sexual;
usually something I've never done and don't want to do
but do find exciting to think about. The more exciting I
find the thought the more I blush. For example, I have
one recurring fantasy in which I dream of being kid-
napped by a gang of motorcyclists who take me with
them and make me their sex slave. They make me do
terrible things and it is something I would hate in real
life but in my fantasy I enjoy it enormously and I know I
blush bright red when I think about it. By the way is it

unusual for a woman my age (I'm 37) to have sexual fantasies?

No one really knows why people blush but the phenomenon is often a result of guilt or fear or anxiety and is commonly triggered off by sexual thoughts of one sort or another. To try to stop yourself blushing begin by making a list of all the things you think about that make you blush. Put the most provocative thoughts, the ones which make you blush most, at the top of the list (for example, your scene with the motorcycle gang) and the least provocative thoughts at the bottom of the list. Then, deliberately bring the thought at the bottom of your list into your mind and try to stay as calm and as relaxed as you can. (It is essential that before you try this you learn a good relaxation technique.) If you feel yourself starting to blush banish the fantasy from your mind and just concentrate on relaxing. When you can think about the least provocative fantasy on your list without blushing move up to the next thought on your list. It'll take some time but eventually you should be able to allow each of your fantasies into your mind while staying so relaxed that you do not blush. I have to warn you that there is one snag: you may find that you enjoy your fantasies less when you can think about them without blushing. Finally, no, its not unusual for women of your age (or any age come to that) to have sexual fantasies. The faraway look in the eyes of the prim lady in the tweed suit in front of you in the supermarket queue may be due to something far more exciting than the price of prunes. Remember that there is frequently no correlation at all between what people fantasise about and what they would enjoy in real life. Some of the fantasies enjoyed by vicars' wives would make a stripper blush. Well, perhaps not. But you know what I mean.

●●

Golf Balls

I work as a golf professional and women at the club where I work often make it pretty clear that they fancy me. So far this year I have been to bed with at least a dozen different women. However, I have now found myself in a difficult position. I was giving a lesson to a woman the other day when she bluntly told me that she wanted me to go back to her home with her. I didn't fancy her at all (she is fat, has a noticeable moustache and smells terrible) so I said 'no' but she shocked me by saying that if I didn't do what she wants she would tell my wife about the other women I've seen. Apparently one or two of the woman have been talking in the women's changing rooms. When I pointed out that this was blackmail she laughed and agreed with me. I think she means business. Can you think of a way I can get out of this?

You have three choices.

1. You can grit your teeth, close your eyes and go to bed with the smelly woman with the moustache (and every other sex starved member who wants to take advantage of your body). If you take this option then within six months you will almost certainly be suffering from permanent impotence. Locker room chatter will quickly destroy your reputation as a stud.

2. You can tell the smelly woman with the moustache to get stuffed with something or someone else and then close your eyes and wait for the sound and feel of bone splintering as your wife lets go with the rolling pin. The physical pain will be as nothing compared to the pain you have to endure when the lawyers start scrubbing your balls clean.

3. You can tell the smelly woman with the moustache to get stuffed and then rush home, confess all to your wife and beg her forgiveness for your twelve accidental indiscretions. You will then spend the next three years putting up shelves, cleaning out the garage and generally becoming a nauseatingly grateful slave to your wife's every whim.

What a pity that you should get bunkered after scoring so well. I'm sure that other readers will share my shallow and unconvincing concern at your predicament. We will all be fascinated to know which of these agonies you choose to endure.

●●●

Expensive Sex

My wife makes me pay money every time I want to have sex with her. I give her what I think is a generous housekeeping allowance but she says that she doesn't particularly enjoy sex so doesn't see why she shouldn't get something out of it. She spends the money on clothes and at the hairdressers. I say that since I'm paying I'm entitled to choose the way we do it but she will only let me do it in the missionary position.

I can't help feeling that you either have sex a hell of a lot or else your wife buys very cheap clothes. How many frocks can you buy for a tenner these days?

I agree with you that you're entitled to choose the way that you have sex with your wife. Since you're paying for sex your physical relationship with your wife has been put on a business footing and you are entitled to have some say over what you get for your money. If she won't budge, and tries to take advantage of her monopoly position, then you should maybe threaten to shop around a little. You might also like to talk about bulk discounts, repeat fees and long term upwards only price reviews. I must say I am terribly impressed by your wife's entrepreneurial instincts. The Government, would be proud of her. Privatising all sexual encounters is bound to figure large in their next manifesto. Your wife could, perhaps, apply to be Minister without Knickers.

●●●

The Prostitute

My husband regularly visits a prostitute who lives near

to us. He spends so much on her that there is not enough left for us to pay rent or housekeeping and although we both have jobs I constantly have to borrow money off my mother and my sister. I have repeatedly asked my husband to stop seeing this woman but he refuses. He says she satisfies him much better than I do in bed. I feel guilty about my inability to make him happy but it hurts me to know that he is with her so often and the shortage of money is making my life unbearable. I get very fed up when I think of him lying in bed with her and then paying her with money I have earned.

Your husband is thoughtless, selfish, unprincipled and contemptible. Leave him. Pack up your belongings and abandon him. He is an evil cad, a foul breathed bounder, an unforgivable blackguard with no redeeming features and a miscreant with the grace of silage. Your life will be brighter, your future rosier and your world more joyful if you wipe the memory of this dark hearted slubberdegullion from your spirit for ever.

●●●

Quite Naked

On an unexpectedly sunny day just before Easter my husband and I stopped our car and went for a walk in what seemed to be a deserted nature reserve. We both felt very romantic and since there didn't seem to be anybody around we got rather carried away. My clothes (including my bra and panties) ended up decorating a small bush and within minutes I was quite naked. Moments later I was astride my husband. The warmth of the sun and the sheer naughtiness of it all enabled me to have a spectacular climax. Afterwards as we walked back along the track leading to our car we passed a large party of bird watchers – all equipped with binoculars. They grinned at us and I knew from the way they looked at me that they had been watching everything. I felt guilty but excited and the memory of it still thrills me.

I wonder if the Great Tit watchers put you down in their little notebooks and if they did how they described you. 'A pair of pink breasted non flying, featherless Bustards. Cock (Lesser Titted) with bald spot, clearly visible curly tuft and perceptible grin and hen (Greater Titted) with exquisitely rounded, bouncy, chest protuberances and curly tuft. Cock and hen were seen mating in woodland. The hen's mating cries ('Oh yes. Oh yes. Oh yes. Now. Now. Oh yes. I'm coming. I'm coming. Oh yes. Oh. Oh that was wonderful.) clearly audible at 200 yards and accompanied by the rhythmic grunting of the male.' You'll probably find yourself listed as a protected species in 'Birds of Europe' next year and if you're really lucky you'll be a 50 point bonus in 'I Spy in the Countryside.' If you're tempted to repeat your adventure be careful: if you feel a birdwatcher's hot breath on your neck or hear a matched pair whispering through the undergrowth I suggest that you slip your knickers back on pretty sharpish and get yourself an agent.

•••

A Fetish For Girdles

I am a young man but I have a fetish for old fashioned ladies girdles. I have fought against the urge to wear one of these for some time but recently I lost the battle. I was standing outside a shop which had girdles in the window when a lady came out from inside and took my hand. She led me into the shop and said that she could see that I was interested in the girdles. I was embarrassed and tried to leave but she grabbed my hand and put a tape measure round my waist. Within minutes I was wearing a girdle and stockings. I really enjoyed it. The lady in the shop wants me to wear girdles for her regularly. I worry that I may be blackmailed if I don't do what she wants. What should I do?

You have to balance the upside against the downside. The upside is that you have a found a way to fulfil your fantasy without hurting anyone – and you have found a woman who is prepared to enjoy your fantasy with you. That sounds pretty good. The downside is that you may end up being embarrassed or losing your job if your secret gets out. Only you can decide how bad that would be.

Surprisingly large numbers of women do enjoy helping men to wear women's clothes. A couple of decades ago women celebrated their liberation from sexual slavery by burning their bras. Now men are celebrating their liberation by wearing bras, girdles and suspender belts.

●●●

Jelly In My Bra

My little girl recently had a birthday party. After all the other children had gone home and my daughter had gone to bed my husband and I started to clear up. There was quite a lot of mess and a lot of food left over. My husband was nagging me about having made too much food when I don't know what came over me but I picked up a handful of blancmange and threw it at him. It landed right in the middle of his shirt front and I couldn't help giggling. He started to shout but then picked up a jelly, came across to where I was standing and pushed it down the front of my blouse and rubbed it into my bra and over my breasts. I then picked up a handful of trifle, undid his trousers and slipped it down inside his underpants. After a few minutes we were both covered in food. My husband undid my blouse and started licking the jelly off my breasts. I felt really sexy and knelt down and started eating up some of the trifle. In the past I've never been very keen on oral sex but licking the trifle off his penis really turned me on. A few moments later we were making love on the carpet. It was fantastic! There was a terrible mess to clear up but it was well worth it. Have you ever heard of anyone doing anything like this before?

You are by no means the first couple to discover the sexual delights of covering one another in food, licking some of it off and then humping through the resultant mess. Slippery, sticky, sweet foods such as custard, cream and syrup seem to be particularly popular with those who get their sexual kicks this way. Recently published, entirely unreliable research shows that 34.6% of the staff working for a major bank enjoy sexually stimulating food fights at least once a month. Oddly enough I've never heard of anyone getting turned on by a food fight with cold gravy or salted porridge (though now that I've said that I've absolutely no doubt that I will be flooded with letters from cold gravy and salted porridge aficionados).

● ●

Lesbian Sex

I am a 22 year old stripper. I work in local pubs and clubs and do shows most evenings. I also do lunchtime shows on Saturdays and Sundays. At one of the pub landlords has asked me to do a show with another girl. He wants us to strip off and pretend to have lesbian sex. Then we're supposed to choose one or two members of the audience, take them on stage and perform sex acts with them. There is always quite a good crowd and the landlord says that most weekends we should be able to find at least one bloke who's got a birthday or a wedding anniversary during the coming week. He says we can't have intercourse with them because that would get him shut down but he says that oral sex is OK. I want to make the men wear condoms but the landlord says that condoms will spoil things and we don't need to bother. I like the taste of semen so I don't mind but do you think it's safe to do it without condoms?

There are over twenty diseases which can be transmitted through sex – and some of these can be transmitted through oral sex. Condoms will provide you with a good degree of protection against most of the nasties and I would certainly recommend that you use them. Maybe you could make putting the condom on as part of your act.

I think I should warn you that if policemen see you performing oral sex on pub customers they will almost certainly charge you, the landlord, the customers and passing motorists with some offence. They will charge you even if no one complains. The police seem to have forgotten why they were originally hired. They have odd priorities these days and prefer to sit in nice warm pubs deliberately allowing themselves to be offended rather than racing around in the rain catching rapists, burglars or vandals.

●●

Driving Me Mad

My wife is driving me mad. She always wants to talk and do things together and doesn't seem to realise that as a bloke I want to spend my evenings and weekends with my mates. She gets plenty of sex because I do it to her three or four times a week whenever I feel the urge. She is getting me down because she cries a lot and if there is one thing I can't stand it is a woman who is always blubbing. I suppose it's her hormones or something and I've told her to get something done about it. Why are women so selfish and demanding?

You sound like the sort of knob rule enthusiast who would be happier with a woman who could be inflated at appropriate moments, and then popped back into a box under the bed when not in use. There is, I suppose, a small chance that in due course you may come to realise that having a meaningful relationship does not begin and end with the unzipping and zipping up again of a well used tool bag. On the other hand there has to be a very good chance that you will remain a complete dickhead for the rest of your life. I rather suspect that you would be doing your wife a good turn if you went to the pub one day and didn't bother to go back home again.

● ●

Porn Stars

How do porn stars make sex last so long? They do it for ages but I can never manage to keep it up for more than five minutes at the most. And how come the man's penis never falls out when they're making love and rolling around on the floor?

Simple: they're only pretending to do it. All that huffing and puffing and screaming and squealing is fake. Porn stars are about as genuine as politicians claiming to be honest, caring and committed. When they fall off the bed, and roll around the room three times the whole thing is more carefully choreographed than professional wrestling. When he nuzzles her ear and batters his groin against her for the 536th time he is whispering: 'Two more minutes of this then when I stiffen and close my eyes you howl like a dog and claw my back. We'll give them long enough for a couple of close ups and then we'll pop down to the canteen for a couple of cheese scones and a nice cup of tea before we film the next one.'

● ●

Climbing The Christmas Tree

I am a widower and very fit. My hobby is gardening. There is a small factory next to my home and one warm day recently the girls who work there exchanged light hearted banter with me as they ate their lunches on the grass. I offered them drinks of tea and later two of the girls came into my garden to bring back the mugs. I was in my shorts and they started teasing me. Things got out of hand and one of the girls ran her hand up my shorts. She received quite a shock since my member is over 12 inches long and has a girth of more than 7 inches. The other girl wanted to look and so we went indoors. Then one thing led to another. It has now become regular practice for some of the girls to come into my home and 'climb the Christmas tree' as they call it. I never thought that women could get so excited by giving themselves pain. They taught me many things – including oral sex. Several of the women now take turns to visit me in the evenings too. I am worried about the possibility of fathering a child. Would this be possible at my age? I feel very guilty about my lapse into libidinousness but I find these assignations difficult to resist. Do you think I am a 'dirty old man'? Should I seek advice to help me conquer these newly aroused urgings?

No, I don't think you're a dirty old man at all. A lucky old man, maybe. But not dirty. It would be perfectly possible for you to father children and so I suggest you buy a large boxful of condoms and use them both to reduce the chances of finding yourself surrounded by unwanted offspring and to limit your own exposure to sexually transmitted diseases. Then I suggest that you build a small altar in your living room and give thanks every evening to the kindly god who endowed you so generously and then put the factory at the bottom of your garden. With these nubile nymphets perched precariously on top of your Christmas tree you have provided adequate proof that there are at least fairies at the bottom of someone's garden.

•••

Breasts

Why are men so interested in women's breasts?

Males are fascinated with breasts from birth. For the first six months of life the interest is inspired by hunger. Interest then wanes for ten or twelve years. When it returns it is inspired by lust.

•••

I Enjoy Wearing Skirts

I am a middle aged man who enjoys wearing skirts. I am a bit bored with just wearing them around the house. I want to go out wearing a skirt. Do you think it would be more acceptable to other people if I put on a wig and make up and tried to look like a woman? I don't want to be a woman and I'm not a pervert I just like wearing feminine clothes. My wife says I should put on a skirt and go out as myself. I would prefer to do this.

If you lived in some other countries (or had been born in a different century) you would be able to go out dressed in a skirt without anyone raising an eyebrow. But I fear that you will be asking for trouble if you try it today. In our guilt laden society there is a real danger that you will be sneered at by the repressed, laughed at by the prejudiced, beaten up by the ignorant and then arrested for causing a breach of the peace. If you want to go out of the house wearing visible feminine clothing you will, I'm afraid, have to do the job properly. The more convincingly you can make yourself look like a woman the smaller the risk of any sort of confrontation.

●●●

The Three Of Us

My boyfriend and his cousin are really close and the three of us spend a lot of time together. One night recently, after an evening at the pub, my boyfriend suggested that his cousin should stay the night with us – in our bed – instead of catching the bus home. He made it pretty clear that they were both going to have sex with me. I was shocked and said 'no'. Since then I've thought about it and have regretted that I refused. My boyfriend hasn't mentioned the idea since but I can't get the thought out of my head. I'm sure my boyfriend would still be keen. And I know his cousin fancies me. Do you think I would be making a mistake if I suggested it?

There's a lot of difference between an exciting sexual fantasy and the sometimes messy, often confusing and invariably 'loaded' consequence of turning that fantasy into reality. I suggest you beware and think carefully. Sharing your body with your boyfriend and his cousin will dramatically change your relationship with your boyfriend, his relationship with his cousin, your relationship with his cousin and his cousin's relationship with you. None of these relationships will ever be the same again. They may be better and they may be worse. But they won't be the same. Not even the cactus on the bathroom shelf will look at you in quite the same way. If you want to change your whole life then maybe a night of fantasy sex will produce dramatic results which you welcome. But if you're happy with things as they are then the price you have to pay for a few hours of sexual adventure could be a high one.

●●●

Giggling In The Showers

What do women talk about in the showers? My girlfriend won't tell me but I can always hear her and the other girls giggling when they're changing.

I am reliably informed by those who know that all women in groups talk incessantly and almost exclusively about sex. Your girlfriend and her chums will be talking (and laughing) about the size, colour and shape of your penis, how often you do it, what sexual fetishes you have, how long you can last and so on. Next time you meet her out of the showers tell her that you overheard the conversation she and the other girls were having and watch her go red!

●●●

Coming Into Money

I work on a market stall twice a week. Afterwards I usually go into the loo and put my takings into my knickers for safety. Last Saturday I got home and found my boyfriend in a randy mood. He had me in the kitchen without giving me time to get undressed. You can imagine my embarrassment when I went to the bank the following Monday.

I believe that this is the first recorded instance of anyone (literally) coming into money.

●●●

My Bruise

While my girlfriend and I were making love I got into a rather tricky position and fell out of bed and banged my head. I had quite a big bruise as a result. Two days later I met three of the girls my girlfriend does aerobics with in a shop in town. One of the girls made a great show of examining my bruise and then told me that in future I should stick to the missionary position. All three of them then laughed and it was clear that my girlfriend had told them exactly what had happened. I was very surprised and embarrassed because I had never realised that women discussed things like sex when talking to one another. I had certainly never guessed that my girl friend would talk about something so intimate to her friends.

B race yourself. Even though they may never have seen you naked your girlfriend's pals could probably identify your penis in the dark. They could probably all draw accurate maps of the veins which stand out when you're excited. And I'll give you long odds that they know all about that time you got drunk and tried on your girlfriend's stockings and suspender belt. I realise that it is sexist and politically incorrect to suggest that there are differences between the sexes but this is one areas where the difference is oceanic in size. Male conversation tends to be confined to solid, straightforward, tangible subjects. Men talk about cars, plumbing and football. Female conversation is usually dominated by intimate details of emotional and physical relationships. Your girlfriend is no different to any other woman.

••

Running Low?

Is it possible to run out of sperm? Masturbating is my favourite hobby and I am worried.

Y ou will not run out of sperm. Indeed, since sperm have a limited shelf life masturbation gets rid of the old ones and makes space available for new, young, vibrant sperm. Because of this masturbation can make a man more fertile! Incidentally, I was impressed the way that you described masturbation as a hobby. I wonder who will be the first celebrity or MP officially to list masturbation among his or her hobbies and interests.

●●

Five Inch High Heels

My husband and I have been married for twelve years and although we both still love each other very much our sex life has been rather low key for quite a while now. Last Wednesday it was our anniversary and my husband suggested that we try something he had read about in one of your books. I dressed up in the tartiest clothes I could find (five inch heeled shoes, see through white blouse, black bra, stockings and suspenders and an obscenely short black skirt) took a taxi into town and sat at the bar of our biggest and smartest local hotel. Twenty minutes later (after I had rejected the advances of two complete strangers who had obviously assumed that I was what I looked like) my husband, who had arrived earlier and had been watching, came and sat down beside me and started to chat me up as though he'd never met me before. After I'd 'let' him buy me dinner and we had flirted with one another outrageously he drove me to a quiet spot and we made love in the back of the car. It was the best sex we'd had for years. The following day a good friend of mine, clearly shocked, telephoned to tell me that she had seen my husband with a hooker. 'The funny thing was,' she said, 'that the woman looked a bit like you. But you should have seen the way she was dressed!' It took me a quarter of an hour to persuade her that the hooker was me! Anyway, I just wanted to thank you – and to let you know that your advice really worked for us.

Congratulations and thanks for letting me know about your successful night out. I've had so many similar letters recently that I'm now a little bit worried that hotel bars up and down the country may become completely clogged with happily married couples pretending to be hookers and tired businessmen – causing all sorts of problems for real hookers and tired businessmen. So, could you all please follow this simple rota system. People whose surnames begin with the letters A to D should try this simple sex game on Mondays. If your surname begins with the letters E to J your night is Tuesday. Wednesday is the night for people whose name begins with the letters K to N. Those of you whose name begins with 0 to S can go out on the town on Thursdays and Fridays are for people with surnames beginning T to Z. We'll leave Saturdays and Sundays for the professionals. And take care. It's a good idea for him to get there before her so that he can make sure nothing gets out of hand.

●●●

She Took Off Her Costume

I recently went into a steam room at the club where I'm a member. I was wearing a pair of swimming trunks. A few minutes later a woman entered. She was in her mid 40s I guess. We were the only two there. After a minute or two she asked if I minded if she took off her costume. She said she would feel more comfortable without it. I am a committee member and reminded her that there is a club rule that members have to stay clothed in the steam room. She pointed out that there was no one else around and that if I didn't mind she certainly didn't. I didn't say anything and so she removed her costume and sat there quite naked. She had a terrific figure but I was terrified that a club official or another committee member might enter.

Coitus Non-interruptus

The polite thing to have done would have been to remove your own bathing trunks. A gentleman never fails to show a lady what he has got when she has shown him what she has got. This traditional and simple law of human behaviour must always take priority over local club rules. You sound like a real prat and a prude to boot. (Why are people who sit on committees always invertebrate, decerebrate and cryptorchid?)

●●●●●●●●●●●●●●●●●●●●●●● ●●●●●●●●●●●●●●●●●●●●●●●●

Coitus Non-interruptus

My wife wants sex all the time.

Your wife is suffering from a rare condition called 'coitus noninterruptus'. According to the results of an unreliable survey of millers, wheelwrights and pawnbrokers, shortly to be conducted, you should think yourself terribly lucky and get stuck in.

●●

Slightly Squiffy

I met my new boyfriend at a party three weeks ago. I usually let a man fondle my breasts on the first date, touch me below the waist on the second date but make him wait until the third date before I let him make love to me, but on this occasion I was so turned on (and slightly squiffy) that I left him do it straight away. We now have sex every time we meet. We hardly ever talk and never go out. Do you think he just wants me for my body?

Sex is the only thing he's after if:

1. He invites you in for coffee and starts getting undressed in the kitchen while waiting for the kettle to boil.
2. He removes your blouse/dress without undoing the buttons.

3. He no longer fondles your breasts before attempting to remove your knickers.

4. He keeps calling you 'darling' or 'love' because he can't remember your name.

5. He has his trousers, shirt and shoes back on before you realise you haven't had an orgasm.

6. He takes his trousers off but keeps his shirt on.

7. You find yourself flat on your back without having had a chance to remove your shoes.

8. You wake up and find he is gone and there is money on the pillow.

9. When you visit him he tells you which position he wants you in before you have taken off your coat.

10. He doesn't bother to unfasten or remove any of your clothes when making love to you.

●●●

Good Christian Parents

We are Good Christian Parents and we strongly object to some of the sexual content of your column, especially since your paper comes out on a Sunday. Some of the letters you print are from depraved people who deserve to rot in hell.

I have received tens of thousands of letters since I started writing this column. Less than half a dozen have been letters of complaint. Three of those have been anonymous letters from people who describe themselves as Good Christian Parents (always with the capital letters). I am reminded of a comment the American musician Frank Zappa made. He pointed out that the Karma Sutra hasn't killed anywhere near as many people as The Bible has. Sexual problems are as much a part of life as indigestion, arthritis and piles. People who describe themselves as Good Christian Parents are now banned from reading this column. Go away.

●●●

A Picture Of My Wife

I was flicking through a soft porn magazine the other day when I came across a picture of my wife. I couldn't believe it! She had posed under another name but it was definitely her. I was shocked. I was also shocked by the comments she was reported to have made. According to the reporter who had interviewed her she had told him that it was her ambition to have sex with an entire football team. In some of the photographs she was wearing bits and pieces of football strip. I didn't even think she liked football.

I shouldn't worry too much about the comments your wife is alleged to have made. There is a good chance that she wasn't even there when she was interviewed but that the writer simply invented something suitably erotic. And if the comments are true then you can take some comfort from the fact that she only wanted to have sex with one team at a time. A less picky and more lascivious woman might have fantasised about both teams, the referee, the two linesmen and even the entire crowd. I assume that since you are one part of the soft porn industry you aren't really too upset about the fact that your wife has played a more active role in the same industry.

●●

Caught Playing With Myself

My mother caught me playing with myself the other day. She slapped me and told me that my fingers will fall off. She also threatened to tell me Dad if she ever catches me at it again.

Stop worrying. You won't lose any fingers. Politicians have all their fingers and they do it professionally. And don't worry too much about your Mum and Dad. I'll bet you a dirty magazine to the

Gross Domestic Output of Germany that they both do it too. You don't think your Dad spends all that time in his garden shed because he likes gardening do you? Rumours about the hazards of masturbation were all started by thin lipped, middle aged women with blue hair and impenetrable two way stretch underwear who think that sex are large bags used by postmen and men delivering coal (As in: 'Don't put those empty sex there, you nasty, little man.')

●●

Unavoidably Aroused

I am a 52 year old married lecturer. Six weeks ago one of my students came to see me for a tutorial. She was wearing very tight jeans and a white blouse. The top four buttons of the blouse were undone and it was quite clear that she was not wearing anything underneath it. I was unavoidably aroused and when, during the tutorial, she made it very clear that she was willing to make love to me I'm afraid that I was foolish enough to succumbed to temptation. She has now told me that unless I give her good marks and ensure that she obtains a good degree she will make a formal complaint about me to the university. If she does this there is a good chance that I will lose my job. I have never done anything like this before and I have no idea what to do now. I would very much appreciate any advice you can give me. I cannot deny that we made love because I have a physical abnormality in a very private place and I know she is aware of this. I have no intention of giving in to her blackmail whatever the consequences. I have thought about complaining to the police but decided against it. If I give her the mark she deserves she will fail though she is a bright student and if she worked hard she could almost certainly pass.

She wants to get her degree and you want to avoid trouble. Why not offer to coach her so that she gets the marks she needs? (But keep your eyes off her cleavage and have your trousers sewn up). In the meantime cover the options by joining a nudist club or taking a lot of showers at a sports club. If you make sure that plenty of strangers have a chance to view your physical abnormality her potentially deadly piece of evidence may shrink in importance.

••

A Bigger Orgasm

Is it true that if you put a small plastic bag filled with ice on a man's scrotum just before he ejaculates he will produce more semen and have a bigger orgasm?

You've been talking to the vicar's wife again, haven't you? In future if you are at a party and you meet a girl clutching a handful of ice you'll know why she has a mysterious Mona Lisa smile.

••

Too Much Sex?

When I got married I was pleased when I discovered that my husband was 'highly sexed'. But I am now becoming increasingly worried. We have sex five times every working day – before we get up, before he goes to work, when he comes home for lunch, when he arrives home from work and when we go to bed. At weekends we have it more often. Although he is 33 his ejaculation seems to go on for several minutes. He is so potent that he can climax up to six times in any one love making session. I am worried about the amount of sperm going into my body. Will it have any long term effect if we continue as we are now?

The average ejaculate contains around 5ml of semen. If your husband ejaculates six times on each occasion when you make love and you make love five times a day then he would, if he produced an average 5ml on each occasion, produce a litre of semen a week. If all that semen stayed where he'd left it then by the end of just one year you would have ten gallons of semen in your body and your whole neighbourhood would smell of horse chestnut blossom.

But I don't think you need worry. Prostitutes cope with heavy sexual activity without blowing up like barrage balloons because gravity ensures that most of the semen trickles out in between love making bouts. This process can be aided by showering and bathing regularly. The enthusiasm of the French for coital sports explains the popularity of the bidet in that country.

You may also be able to gain some slight consolation from the thought that your husband's production of semen will be almost certainly be rather less than that of a less sexually active individual.

• •

Erotic Feelings

I have erotic feelings about cars. I only have to look at a car I find attractive to get an erection.

I assume that you only find certain makes of car a turn on. Ferraris and Lambourghinis are fairly sexy vehicles but I can't really see anyone get turned on by a Vauxhall Vulva or a Ford Smegma. Try and make sure that you don't chase after cars. This can be a humiliating experience. If you do catch a car remember that the exhaust pipe, however attractive it may appear to be, is likely to be very hot.

• •

Lonely And Miserable

My husband has been working away from home for several weeks and I've been a bit lonely and miserable recently. Last Saturday a girlfriend, whose husband is in the forces and also working away from home, asked me to go into town with her for a drink. We dressed up a bit (short skirts, see through blouses and stockings and suspenders) and went to a pub I'd never been to before. There was a band playing there that my girl-friend wanted to listen to. I had a few drinks and got quite tipsy, though I have to admit I wasn't drunk and I did know what I was doing.

My girl friend is a bit of a flirt and we got picked up by four lads; all of whom were quite a lot younger than us. When the pub closed we went back to a flat with them and carried on drinking and dancing.

I was sitting talking to two of the boys when I looked round and saw that my friend was kissing one of the lads and letting another fondle her below the waist. As I watched the one who was kissing her undid her blouse and took out her breasts and the other one pushed up her skirt and pulled down her knickers. Like me she was wearing stockings not tights. She didn't try to stop them at all and to my amazement she started making love to the two lads at the same time. She was naked from the waist up but still had on her stockings and suspender belt. I had never seen anything like it and I found myself feeling quite turned on.

When one of the boys I was talking to started to fondle my breasts I didn't do anything to stop him and a few moments later I was kneeling beside her on the carpet making love to two boys whose names I didn't even know. We stayed the night and both made love to all four of the lads several times. One of them had a much bigger thing than anything I've ever seen before but to my surprise it didn't hurt at all; in fact I had in-credible orgasms when he put it in me.

They didn't use condoms but I'm not worried because I know I can't get pregnant because I'm on the pill. I am, however, worried sick that my husband will find out though I think I'm probably safe because the pub was in a part of town that we never usually go to. Do you think I should write and tell my husband what happened?

You might not have to worry about being pregnant but you should worry about being infected. I think you'd be wise to pop along to the Sexually Transmitted Disease clinic at your local hospital and ask them to check you out.

I don't think you should write and tell your husband.

What the hell were you going to say?

'Dear John,

I hope you are well. The weather hasn't been very good. The grass needs cutting. I met four blokes in a pub and made love to them all. One of them had a very big penis – much bigger than yours. The garage roof is leaking and I had a cold last week.

Love

Your wife

You wouldn't be normal if you didn't feel guilty and apprehensive. But I'm afraid that's the price you have to pay for your night out. Neither you nor your husband have anything to gain from a burst of honesty on your part.

•••

Scared Stiff

My boyfriend's erection is not very firm. Do you have any suggestions to make?

Next time you are planning to make love stand behind him and shout 'boo'. This should scare him stiff.

•••

Fantastic Condition

I work as a personal trainer. I visit my clients at home or in their offices. I recently acquired a new client – a married woman in her early forties. She is in fantastic condition and has a gorgeous figure. After a recent workout she asked me to give her a massage. She stripped off and lay down on the floor. After massaging her back, her arms, her legs and, at her request, her buttocks, I had the shock of my life when she sat up, threw away her towel and lay down on her back – stark naked. She then asked me to massage her chest. When I hesitated she gently took my hand and put it on one of her breasts and told me to be gentle. While I very slowly and gently massaged her breasts she reached into my shorts and started to play with me. Moments later she reached up and pulled my shorts down to my ankles. The sex was incredible. Do you think it would be ethical for me to see her again?

I confess that I wasn't aware that personal trainers were expected to subscribe to a code of ethics. Are you really likely to be hauled in front of a committee of pin striped incontinents and stripped of your gym shoes and tee shirt if you continue to provide your client with a more than usually comprehensive work-out? Assuming that neither of you have regular partners of your own, and that you take the usual precautions to avoid infection and pregnancy, the big question you have to ask yourself is: Do I continue to charge this woman for my services? Maybe a suitable compromise would be to charge her for the time you spend with your shorts on but provide shorts-off services as a perk. I don't think you need worry too much about what you are doing. After all, most big companies now provide a similar service. Every day, all over the country, millions of customers hand over money and get screwed.

●●●

My Girlfriend Passed Out

While making love to my girlfriend recently she passed out. She came round again after half a minute and told me not to worry. She said it happened a lot to her. I've never come across this before, have you?

I have no personal experience of this phenomenon but it's known as the 'little death' and is quite common – particularly among women. Some individuals have a sort of semi fit. Others just drift into unconsciousness. It can be very scary for the partner who remains awake. Individuals who pass out regularly should warn new partners to avoid the embarrassment of coming to in an ambulance.

●●●

Shall I Go All The Way?

My boyfriend wants me to make love to some of his friends and I don't know what to do. Every Saturday evening he and a group of four or five mates go out for a curry together. They usually come back to our flat afterwards. Two or three weeks ago my boyfriend insisted on showing a video he'd taken when we were on holiday in Spain. The video included several shots of me topless on the beach. The video went down very well and when my boyfriend suggested that I show off my boobs for real I did. I didn't want to at first but I'd had quite a lot to drink and they were all egging me on. Now my boyfriend wants me to let his mates all have sex with me. I really don't want to but my boyfriend says that after I bared my boobs his pals are expecting me to go all the way with them.

Tell your boyfriend that you think that exposing your breasts was a mistake. Then arrange to spend the next few weekends with your mother/sister/best-friend/aunt in Cleethorpes/Sunder-land/Bristol/Dover.

If your boyfriend still tries to insist that you have sex with his chums I suggest that you trade him in for something more sensitive. This won't be difficult. A vibrator would be more sensitive.

●●●

The Boy Across The Street

Every evening at eleven o'clock I undress, have a shower and get ready for bed. I've never bothered to draw the curtains. Two months ago I looked out of my window and noticed that a boy who lives across the street was watching me. Since then I've seen him watching me every evening. I still don't draw the curtains and I confess I make my strip tease last as long as possible, frequently posing in front of the window in my undies or sometimes just my knickers. I find it quite exciting knowing that he is watching my every move. Ten days ago he stood up and I could see that he was masturbating so I started playing with myself too. We now do the same thing every evening. We are both sixteen and go to the same school but when we see one another in the street we just say 'hello'. I think he is a rather shy person. I know I am very shy. Is what we are doing illegal or dangerous?

Unless you both open your windows and he manages to fire his semen through his window, across the street, through your window and into a position from which the sperm could swim into your vagina (you would probably have to be standing on your head at the time for this to happen) you need not worry too much about either pregnancy or infection. You are practising safe sex. The main danger to you is that your across the street partner (or some other observer) may be so excited by your nightly show that he is driven to accost you in the street. As far as the law is concerned I suspect that the boy across the street may risk double jeopardy. He could be arrested as a peeping tom (for watching you) and for exposing himself to you. The law is a little dotty in this area (as it is in so many other areas) and the boy across the street could end up buried deeply in the brown sticky stuff. With this in mind maybe you would like to think about the possibility of one day allowing your relationship to develop into something a little more private. You do not have to take your relationship to the immediate and obvious physical conclusion: since you are both shy you may find that holding hands and sharing kisses is, in its own way, even more exciting than what you are doing at the moment.

●●●

Husband In The Wardrobe

When my husband found out that I was having an affair he didn't react as I had expected. Instead of being jealous, angry or upset he was desperate to find out more. He made me tell him everything my lover and I had done together. Now he wants me to take other lovers – as long as I tell him everything that happens. He even wants to hide in our wardrobe and secretly watch me making love.

As a highly trained professional observer of human frailties I can tell you that your husband harbours deep seated homosexual inclinations which he is unprepared to acknowledge on a conscious level. He is having sex with men through you and at the same time punishing himself and expiating his guilt. Translated into the vernacular this means that your old man is a kinky bastard who gets his rocks off watching you sucking and screwing your way through the local male population. You can minimise the more obvious physical hazards by buying condoms wholesale – and using them. The possible mental and emotional consequences of your new lifestyle are legion but there are no rules which say that your relationship with your husband will not thrive under these unusual circumstances.

●●●

Constant Erections

I read your reply to a letter about nudism with great interest. My wife wants me to join her nudism club but I have constant erections when I think about going there – I hate to think what would happen if I actually **went** there. Is there anything medical I could take to stop me being aroused?

I can think of dozens of drugs that would stop you being aroused. The snag is that most of them would probably also stop you breathing and make your hair fall out. To be honest I don't think you need worry. You may *think* that you would find a visit to a nudist colony irresistibly stimulating but I doubt if the sight of 99 year old naked women playing ping pong would provoke autonomic verticalisation of your fertilisation equipment. (Sorry about that. The euphemistic phrase is there because the Editor says I can't use the words 'penis' or 'erection' in case I offend Mrs W of Milton Keynes again. Whoops. I have. Now I'll probably get fired. Will you miss me?)

●●●

She Had Her Knickers Off Before I'd Boiled The Kettle

I had a date with a beautiful girl last Saturday. I really fancied her – and, she fancied me too! We got back to my place and she had her knickers off before I'd boiled the kettle but even though I wanted her so badly that my balls ached I just couldn't get it up. I was mortified. It has never happened to me before. What I can't understand is that I wanted her more than I've ever wanted any other woman. I rushed to my doctor on Monday morning but he said there was nothing wrong with me. He just sort of laughed and said it was one of those things that happen. I don't think there is anything wrong with the equipment because I had the biggest boner I've ever had two days later. But why did it happen?

Probably because you were too anxious to succeed! The penis is a wilful little beast with a mind of its own and the chances are that it simply decided to show you who is boss. Knowing how desperate you were to perform well it downed tools. I suggest that next time you try to relax a little, take your time and spend a little longer on foreplay before you get down to the nitty gritty of lovemaking.

••

A Womaniser

I have worked for my present boss for seven years as his personal assistant/secretary. He is quite a womaniser and I have often had to lie for him when his wife has rung up wanting to speak to him. He often tells her he is working and then goes to a hotel with one of his mistresses. Last week, however, things reached a new low. On Thursday he asked me to go to his home to pretend to be his wife. He said that one of his mistresses had told him that on that evening she was going to go round to his home, confront his wife and tell her what had been going on. My boss is frightened of his wife finding out about his affairs because he knows that the alimony would cripple him. He wanted me to pretend to be his wife and to sit there while his mistress explained what a double crossing bastard he is. He said it would be easy to do because the mistress has never seen his wife. Moreover he said that his wife would be out for the whole of that evening attending a Parent Teachers meeting.

I am now very ashamed of the fact that I did what he wanted. I went to his home. I pretended to be his wife. And I listened as his mistress opened her heart. She was very dignified though I could tell that she was close to tears.

I feel disgusted with myself for doing this and I have already decided that I intend to find another job as soon as possible. I felt very sorry for the mistress because I know that my boss has lied to her many times before. He is a real bastard and he is dragging me down to his level.

Do you think I should tell his mistress and his wife the truth about him?

No. They won't thank you for telling them the truth. Leave your boss, as quickly as you can (or even quicker if possible). Without your protection maybe the women in his life will find out the truth about him. Maybe you could plant a few 'time bombs'. Slip a condom or something lace and flimsy into his jacket pocket and leave him to do some wriggling on his own.

●●●

What Do Lesbians Do?

We live next door to two women. I am sure they are lesbians. What do lesbians do together?

What a daft question. What do heterosexuals do together? Watch TV? Eat spaghetti with a side salad? Play scrabble? Hoover the stairs and plump up the cushions in the living room? Sew on loose buttons, feed the cat, water the plants and listen to music? If they are lesbians (and just because they live together that doesn't mean that they are) and are in love with one another then they probably also do all sorts of exciting sexual things to one another when you're not looking. And if you haven't got the imagination to work out for yourself what they do then I think you should remain ignorant. You sound an odious, nosy little toe rag and I think you should get back to masturbating in the lavatory with a copy of your wife's underwear catalogue perched on your knees.

●●●

A Pretty Doctor

My doctor is a very pretty woman in her thirties. I believe she is divorced. I had to see her last week for a medical examination. While I lay on the couch naked she unbuttoned her white coat. She told me that this was because she was feeling very hot. She said the central heating had gone out of control. She was wearing just underwear beneath the white coat – a purple bra and pantie set and a matching suspender belt with purple stockings. When she put her hands on my skin I got very aroused and responded in the traditional way almost instantly. When she saw my erection she couldn't take her eyes off it. She asked me if the erection was her fault. When I said I thought it probably was she said she felt very guilty and asked me if I wanted her to deal with it. She wrapped her fingers around it, licked her lips and made it pretty clear what she meant. I felt very embarrassed and muttered something about not wanting to trouble her. She then became very abrupt and professional and fastened her coat up again. She performed the examination in about two minutes and long before she had finished my erection had melted like a snowman in a heatwave. She seemed rather offended and hardly spoke to me when she wrote out my sick note. Now I regret my shyness. I would very much like to have a second chance. How do you think I should go about this?

How nice it is to know that there are still doctors around who think that their patients should come first. Technically women doctors are regulated by the same ethical rules as those which prevent men from having sexual relationships with their female patients but I think you can safely leave that particularly worry to your doctor. She is, after all, paid to take responsibility.

If you think your saucy doctor in purple underwear was expressing an interest in a relationship with you then you could ring her up or drop her a note asking her out. If, on the other gland, you feel that her interest was purely physical you could simply visit the surgery again (armed with a supply of condoms) and be honest with her – tell her that you very much regret your shyness and that if her offer still stands you would like to take her up on it.

If her face lights up and the white coat buttons start flying across the room you can safely assume that your lucky day has arrived.

If she remains cold and aloof you can equally safely assume that either you misinterpreted her intentions or else she is still feeling a little hurt at having been rejected.

●●●

Great Things

My girlfriend is 18. She has a 44 inch bust. She wants to go into modelling.

I am sure she has great things in front of her.

●●●

Shouting Out

When my husband and I make love I often shout out loud and make a lot of other noises. We have been invited to stay with friends for the New Year but I'm a bit worried. Is there anything I can do to make sure that I don't make any embarrassing noises while we're there? (There will be quite a lot of other people staying there at the same time).

Take a good book with you and ask your hostess for single beds and two hot water bottles.

• •

Wet Dream

Last night I had a wet dream. I dreamt that I was making love to one of the weather girls off the television. It is a long time since I had sex and it was wonderful – even if it was only a dream. I dreamt that the girl performed oral sex on me and it was terrific. How can I make sure that I have another dream like this?

There is no way to guarantee a repeat performance but you can increase your chances of success by making sure that you are thinking about a suitable weather girl as you drop off to sleep. There are, as far as I am aware, no laws against this yet though I expect that politicians are working on it so don't tell anyone else your secret.

• •

I Dress In Provocative Clothes

I am female, single and in my thirties. I live alone and usually dress and behave quite sensibly and demurely.

67

I Dress In Provocative Clothes

About a year ago I discovered a new pleasure. I put on a long wig and lots of make up, dress up in very provocative clothes and then go for a walk around our local town centre. I usually do this on a Saturday evening and I get a real thrill from the wolf whistles and shouts of approval. I have steadily become more and more daring. A week ago I went out in a red PVC skirt, fishnet stockings and suspenders and a tiny, black jacket with no bra underneath. I wore lots of make-up and four inch heels. The attention I got was unbelievable. Many men made suggestions to me. I had my skirt lifted at one point and another man 'accidentally' bumped into me and handled my breast. Two motorists stopped their cars and propositioned me. Tipsy with excitement I unfastened the buttons on my jacket and walked home with my breasts bobbing about quite bare. I am now contemplating going out without bra or pants. I am petrified of being recognised or getting into trouble with the police but I know that I will not be able to resist the temptation. Can I be arrested for dressing provocatively? I don't want to stop being an exhibitionist but I do feel that I perhaps need to control myself.

Being arrested is not your greatest danger. There is a real risk that if you continue exhibiting yourself in this way you will be attacked or raped. I strongly suggest that instead of going out onto the streets dressed in the way you describe you find a 'fetish' club where you can dress up as tartily as you like and enjoy yourself in safety. There is absolutely nothing at all wrong with being an exhibitionist – it sounds as though it is, for you, a valuable expression of a previously hidden part of your personality – but you must be more careful about where, and to whom, you exhibit yourself.

●●

Every Time I Do This He Gets An Erection

I regularly cut my husband's hair with electric clippers. Every time I do this he gets an erection. Now he wants me to cut his hair every few days. He has hardly any hair left and people are beginning to ask questions.

Take the cutting blade out of the clippers or try cutting the hair other people cannot see (but do take care around the twiddly bits). I am afraid that you may now be committed to cutting your husband's hair for the rest of his life. If for some reason he absolutely must visit a hairdresser remind him to wear baggy trousers and to carry a newspaper.

••

Swallow

My boyfriend wants me to have oral sex with him but I am afraid of putting his penis in my mouth because when he ejaculates I may end up swallowing his semen. Will I have to have to have my stomach pumped out if he does this?

No. Unless your boyfriend has any infection or the semen goes down the wrong way and you choke (very unlikely) the risks associated with oral sex are very small. Indeed, semen contains a variety of useful nutrients – including phosphorus, potassium, sodium, calcium, magnesium, zinc, protein, fructose and vitamins C and E – and some people believe that a regular intake of the stuff may improve your health.

••

I Like To Fondle

I like to fondle my girlfriend's breasts but some days she won't let me. I say that since we are living together

I have a right to touch them whenever I want to but she says that I don't. I say that she says this because she has been listening to women's libbers. What do you say?

I say you big heap lump of stale boil oozings. What you say if your girl friend say she have the right to squeeze your balls tightly every time she feels like it?

Has it occurred to you that the two lumps on your girl friend's chest are actually part of her body? Has it crossed your tiny, pimple sized mind that having your welding gloves kneading her tender bits may occasionally be painful?

No, I don't suppose it has.

Why don't you buy yourself a rugby ball, cut it into two and stick the two halves onto your sting vest. That way you'll have a pair of breasts you can fondle all day long.

• •

Noisy Sex

Is it acceptable for a woman to make a noise during sex? When my boyfriend makes love to me I frequently feel like shouting out but I try to keep quiet because it somehow doesn't seem ladylike to make a noise. Do you think he would mind if I let myself go a little more?

I doubt very much if he would mind. An entirely unreliable recent survey of retired civil servants showed that 83.7% of them preferred noisy sexual partners. Favourite phrases included: 'Do it to me!', 'Yes, yes, big boy!' and 'Oh, my God, I'm coming, I'm coming!'. Many men like their partners to use words which would not be considered appropriate for use in the drawing room. And it is not at all uncommon for some very refined women to use earthy four letter words at moments of high passion. Please don't feel shy or embarrassed about showing your feelings in the bedroom. The average man's dream woman has been described as someone who can be a cook in the kitchen, a house keeper around the home and a whore in the bedroom.

• •

Having The Boss For Dinner

Last weekend my husband brought his boss home with him for dinner. I knew he was coming and had really made an effort and prepared a lovely meal. I spent a whole week's housekeeping budget on the food and wine. After the meal I sat on the sofa next to my husband's boss and while we were talking he casually put his arm around me and started stroking my shoulder and slipping his fingers inside my blouse. I didn't like to say anything because I know that he has a lot of power over my husband's career but as soon as I could I went out into the kitchen to fetch more coffee. While I was there my husband came in and told me that he had a headache and was going to bed. He asked me to stay up to entertain his boss! I was very surprised. My husband doesn't normally get headaches and even if he had had a stinker I would have thought he would have soldiered on in order to try and make a good impression on his boss. 'You've made a real hit with him,' whispered my husband. 'He really fancies you so be nice to him!' At that point I suddenly realised what was going on. I asked my husband if he expected me to have sex with his boss. I was absolutely flabbergasted when he told me that it was up to me but that it would do his career a lot of good if I did. I didn't know what to do and so when my husband went back upstairs I was in quite a daze when I went back into the living room with two cups of coffee. The coffee never got drunk. My husband's boss had my clothes off in less than five minutes and he had sex with me twice. After he had gone home I stayed downstairs alone and couldn't believe what had happened. I felt really ashamed of myself and very dirty. But I have to admit that I found the sex very exciting. When he started taking my clothes off I didn't show him any encouragement but I quickly got excited and it showed. I never usually have orgasms when my husband makes love to me but I didn't have any trouble having orgasms with his boss. When my husband eventually crept downstairs to see how things had gone I screamed abuse at him. That was over a week ago. I now feel very confused. I have told my husband that if he ever tries to put me in a position like that again I will leave him. But I can't forget what happened and I have an awful feeling that if a similar situation occurred again I would not put up any resistance. I almost feel like a whore.

You are a whore. And your husband is a pimp. Having successfully managed the deed why be afraid of the words? Since your aim in making love to your husband's boss was at least partly to improve or secure your husband's wage packet you were screwing for money: that makes you a whore. A potentially high class hooker, but a hooker nevertheless.

I have deliberately been blunt because I think that you have to face reality if you are to decide how best to deal with what has happened and what seems certain to happen again.

Did you really 'allow' your husband's boss to have sex with you because you were in a daze? I think that is a rather weak claim. I suspect that the first reaction of most women would have been to try to brain their husband with a kitchen implement. Are you really so weak and insipid that you simply lay down and opened your legs? Would you unquestioningly do anything for your husband rather than disappoint him? Or did you go to bed with this man because you realised that a promotion for your husband would mean a bigger wage packet? Or did you, perhaps, agree to what happened because you were excited by the prospect of having sex with a virtual stranger? Did the knowledge that your husband was upstairs make the whole incident even more exciting?

And what about your husband? Was he liberal with your favours simply to further his own career? Or was he turned on by the knowledge of what was happening? Is he going to want to watch next time?

Only when you are both honest with yourselves about what has already happened will you be able to decide how best to deal with the next time. And one way or another I am pretty sure that there will be a next time.

Finally, I have a question for you. Did your husband get promoted? Or did his boss screw you both?

•••

Sex With My Mother-in-Law

My wife has a very important job. Two weeks ago she went abroad for five days to attend a conference. I'm not very good at cooking and household chores – though I always do more than my fair share in the garden to make up for this – so while she was away her mother offered to come and stay to look after me. Although my mother in law is in her late forties – nearly twenty years older than me – she is very attractive and still has a terrific figure. Nevertheless I had never thought of her in any sexual way and it was quite a shock to me when, on our first evening alone, she sat down beside me on the sofa to watch TV and I realised that I was aroused by her presence. She was wearing a very short skirt which had ridden up her thighs and had on a tight sweater and a flattering bra. When she casually rested her hand on my leg I started to sweat as I realised that I was developing an enormous and very noticeable erection. I quickly picked up the newspaper and dropped it across my lap to hide the evidence. 'You don't have to be embarrassed,' she said, tossing the newspaper aside and smiling at me. 'I'm really very flattered.' By the way she was looking at me it was obvious she wanted me to kiss her. A few minutes later our son-in-law/mother-in-law relationship had been changed for ever. We slept together in the spare bed until my wife came back. Now that my wife is back home I'm torn. I know my mother in law is keen to repeat our experience but I'm worried about damaging my marriage. My wife is going away to another conference next month and once again her mother has offered to come and look after me. Help! What do I do?

First of all you have to decide whether you want this affair to stop or to carry on. If you want it to stop then you should talk confidentially to your mother in law and explain to her that you enjoyed making love to her very much but that you are frightened of wrecking your marriage. Ask her to find some reason not to come and stay while your wife is away and buy yourself a cookbook. If you can't say 'no' and you want your dangerous affair to carry on then you're going to have to be very careful to make sure that your wife doesn't find out because discovering that her mum and her hubby have been bonking each other's brains out in the guest room is likely to send her off into orbit. You should also make sure that your diet contains plenty of protein and zinc.

●●

A Large Dildo For Christmas

I bought my girlfriend a large dildo for Christmas. She has now started 'wearing' it every day. She puts it inside and keeps it in place with her panties. She says that by contracting her vaginal muscles she can have tremendous orgasms whenever she wants. She works in a bank and if I pop in during opening hours I can tell by the look in her eyes that she's having another quick one.

Next time I visit a bank I shall study the female tellers with greatly enhanced interest – looking for any with a 'far-away' look. Trying to spot the teller with the dildo will make queuing a positive pleasure. It's nice to know that dreamy eyed bank clerks have more to get excited about than deposits, withdrawals and standing orders.

● ●

Blazing Row

I had a blazing row with my boyfriend, threw my engagement ring at him and went back to my flat feeling furious. When I got there my flatmate and her boyfriend were watching a blue movie. I sat down with them and had a few drinks. The movie was about a man and two women and we started off by giggling but soon I realised that my friend had unzipped her boyfriend's trousers and was stroking an enormous erection. To my astonishment she looked at me and said: 'There's enough here for two. Do you want some?' I thought 'Why not?' and joined in. We did everything the people on the video had done and it was the most exciting experience of my life.

A few days later my flat mate's boyfriend brought another movie round. He also brought a friend. I was still feeling angry with my boyfriend – particularly since he hadn't been in touch with me at all. The inevitable result was that the four of us all had sex together.

Now my boyfriend wants us to make up. I don't want him to know what happened but my flatmate keeps giggling and making oblique references to what went on. I am scared that she will say too much. I would confess but I know that my boyfriend will never forgive me if he finds out what happened. He has a foul temper and is very possessive.

Are you sure you are ready for a long term relationship? And if you are, then are you sure that your current boyfriend is the right person for you to be involved with? If you answer 'yes' to both those questions then maybe you need to think about changing flats or flatmates in order to preserve your secret. If you answer 'no' then your course of action is fairly clear: keep your flatmate and tell your boyfriend that you're not interested in a reconciliation.

• •

Team Dream

Last night I dreamt that I made love to the other ten players in my husband's football team while he simply stood and watched. I have had this dream several times since I have been pregnant. Is this anything I should be worried about? (I feel rather guilty about it because I seem to enjoy myself in the dream).

I'm tempted to ask if your husband is the goal-keeper because it certainly sounds as if he doesn't score very often. But I won't. I bet you've been avoiding sex because your doctor has warned you that sex could damage your pregnancy (though sex isn't normally a threat to a healthy baby). Because you aren't allowed to have sex with your husband you're having sex with men other than your husband in your dreams. Simple – and absolutely nothing at all for you to worry about or feel guilty about. Enjoy your dream.

• •

Nurse's Outfit

Two years ago my husband, Geoff, bought me a skimpy nurse's outfit for our anniversary. I put it on to please him and it certainly seemed to get him very excited. Since then he has bought me quite a variety of sexy clothes including a French maid's costume and several bras which have holes for my nipples to poke through. I don't mind wearing these clothes for him but he now wants me to serve dinner in my French maid's costume when two business contacts of his come to our home next week. The skirt is so short that it barely covers my bottom and the top is so low cut that if I bend forward my breasts (which are quite large) fall out. I'm worried that the visitors might get the wrong idea but Geoff says it'll help break the ice and might help him get an important order. When I objected he pointed out that I have worn more revealing clothes on the beach. I couldn't think of an answer to that because he was, of course, absolutely right. What do you think?

I don't think Geoff is as interested in getting an important order as he is in displaying your assets to his guests. Say 'no' unless you want to be served up as the spécialité de la maison. Make it clear that while you don't mind dressing in revealing clothes for him you don't want strangers feasting on your nibbly bits when they should be nibbling on your feasty bits. There is a lot of difference between wearing a revealing bikini on the beach and wearing a revealing skimpy costume in front of a couple of guests in your own home.

● ●

Always On The Look-out

Once a month my wife and I attend a party. After a few drinks everyone puts on a blindfold and then strips off.

The host and hostess (who do not put on blindfolds but do take off their clothes) write all the mens' names on pieces of paper. The blindfolded ladies then pick their partners. Each male and female pairing are then led to a part of the house where they can make love. When we've all finished we return to the living room, have coffee and something to eat and try to guess who we've made love to. (My wife picked out my name once but we weren't disappointed.) We are always on the look out for new couples. The only rules are that men must always wear a condom and no anal sex is allowed. I'm sure that if my family and workmates knew what we do they would be shocked but we're not hurting anyone.

People say that television has killed home entertainment and the art of conversation but your letter proves that this is certainly not the case. It's wonderful to know that in your community the spirit of brotherly (and sisterly) love still runs strong. In Victorian times friends and neighbours would gather around the piano, sing hymns, exchange embroidery tips and play hunt the thimble. These days friends and neighbours strip naked, lie on top of the piano, play hide the thimble and sing out 'Hallelujah!' So little has changed.

●●

Twins

A few months ago when my husband's twin brother was thrown out of his home he came to stay with us. On his first night both men stayed out late. When he finally came to bed my husband woke me up and made passionate love to me. Early the next morning I woke up and realised that it was my brother in law and not my husband who was in bed with me. Later, while I pretended to be asleep, my brother in law left and my husband got into bed and had sex with me. Since then this has been happening frequently. I can't say that I mind and even without the sex with my brother in law I am having far more sex than I got before he moved in. Should I tell them that I know what they are up to?

That depends largely upon whether or not you mind things changing. Because if you speak up then things will probably change.

When they know that you know what is going on they may both be very embarrassed. The result could be an instant and dramatic reduction in your nookie ration. Or they may suggest an escalation. And you could end up playing a highly erotic version of piggy in the middle.

Somehow, I get the impression that you rather like the present situation. So I suggest that (apart from the usual moaning and groaning at appropriate moments) you keep quiet.

(I assume, by the way, that you are aware of the emotional and physical dangers of sharing your favours in this way.)

• •

Small Penis

I think the secret of a happy life is to find a partner who likes you the way you are and then relax. My penis is about three inches long but if a woman doesn't like it she can sod off.

Thank you for sharing this with us. Actually, although you have chosen a simple way in which to express a complex series of philosophical thoughts I think you're absolutely spot on. Psychiatrists, psychotherapists and counsellors would all be out of work if everyone had these two sentences tattooed on their foreheads at birth. Oh, all right, I'm exaggerating but you know what I mean.

• •

Peeping Tom

My husband was given a telescope for Christmas. He has set it up in our bedroom and although he claims that he is using it to look at the stars I think he spends most of his time watching the women across the road getting undressed at night. We live opposite a small block of flats and you can see into quite a few rooms from our bedroom. One woman in particular seems a special favourite. I've seen her myself without a telescope. She is divorced and aged about 45. She has a rather voluptuous figure. She always gets undressed with the curtains open and the light on and I don't think she would complain. I suspect she knows exactly what is going on. But she's not the only one and although I don't think my husband means any harm I'm worried that he could get into serious trouble.

You should firmly dissuade your husband from continuing with his newly formed one man Neighbourhood Watch scheme.

The law is rather sexist about this sort of thing. If a man strips off and is seen getting undressed in his own bedroom by a woman then he can be arrested for exhibitionism, lewd behaviour or, depending on his personal endowment, possession of lethal weapon 1, 2 or 3.

On the other hand if a woman strips off in her bedroom and a man who doesn't have an official invitation sees her doing it then he can be arrested as a peeping tom.

If one of the unwilling starlets in your husband's private milky way catches a glimpse of him flashing his telescope at her then the second hand food could really hit the whirling blades. And even though you suspect that voluptuous neighbour is an enthusiastic participant in your husband's Neighbourhood Watch scheme there is a real danger that she may too may turn him in and recommend him for a porridge diet and a job repairing mailbags.

All things considered I think you'd both be better off if you took the telescope back to the shop and got them to swap it for a train set.

● ●

The Show Must Go On

My girlfriend and I live in a very small basement flat. We had always assumed that our bedroom was invisible from the pavement but two days ago we discovered that passers by can look straight in and see exactly what we are doing. A man in a local pub told me that he and several mates always walk past our flat on the way home so that they can watch us getting ready for bed and making love. My own first reaction was anger but my girlfriend admitted that she found the knowledge that she has been watched rather a turn on and she has suggested that we continue to leave our curtains open so that the show can go on. Would this be legal?

Your generosity towards these sad voyeurs, whose own lives are so empty that they need to get their kicks second hand, by peering through your windows, is commendable. Personally, I feel that you both deserve awards in the next Honours List. An MBE each would be richly deserved. However, I must warn you that your proposal is almost certainly against the law. Under new legislation any activity which gives pleasure but does not involve cruelty is punishable by a heavy fine, transportation to the Antipodes or both.

Incidentally, a rather similar thing happened to me many years ago. I was a medical student and going out (or rather, staying in) with a nurse. Because she was working nights we used to meet in her room in the nurses' home at ten o'clock every morning and make love. We made love without bothering to get into the bed and because her room was on the sixth floor we never wasted time closing the curtains. One morning I was late getting away from the main hospital building and as I hurried along the corridor on the ninth floor I found the way blocked by a group of doctors, nurses and orderlies crowding around a window. As I tried to squeeze past to get to the lift I asked a friend what was going on. He told me that they all gathered there every morning at ten to watch a couple having sex on the sixth floor in the nurses' home. I pushed my way to the front and found I could look right down into my girlfriend's bedroom. She was lying on her back on top of her bed – quite naked. 'We're going to try and find out who her boyfriend is today,' a medical registrar told me, brandishing a pair of binoculars. 'Up until now all we've ever seen of him is his bum.' My girlfriend was startled when, a few minutes later, I rushed into her room and, instead of simply tearing my clothes off and leaping on top of her, I lunged straight at the windows and drew the curtains.

●●

Over His Knee

My husband and I had a steaming row the other evening. Eventually he got so cross that he picked me up, put me over his knee, pulled down my jeans and spanked my bottom. I was fighting as hard as I could but he is much taller and stronger than I am and I couldn't free myself. At first I felt humiliated and angry but much to my surprise I found that I became sexually aroused. He obviously did too and when he eventually stopped spanking me we had really good sex. Is there anything strange or unhealthy about this? I feel rather guilty about it but wouldn't mind trying it again sometime and don't know how to suggest it.

There isn't anything strange or unhealthy about it. They do it all the time in Belgium. If you want to try it again why not just try being deliberately naughty? And then when he looks at you sternly you can say (with wide open eyes, fluttering eyelashes and a feigned look of terror): 'Oh dear, you're not going to spank me again, are you?'

• •

Roman Holiday

My husband and I recently went to Rome for our 5th wedding anniversary. On our first evening there, while I was looking out of the hotel window admiring the view, my husband came up behind me and stood beside me caressing my bottom. I was wearing a very thin silky dress and we both got quite turned on. Before I knew what was happening he had pulled down my knickers, pushed up my dress, moved behind me and unzipped his trousers. We then made love with me leaning on the window sill and him standing behind me. I found it very exciting, particularly because I was in full view of the people passing by just below our window. Although no one could see anything they shouldn't have seen I suspect that quite a few people knew exactly what we were doing. We repeated this experience twice and on one occasion, at night, I stood in the window naked while my husband made love to me from behind. I found making love in public very exciting. Since coming home we have made love in the park, on a train, in a multi storey car park and in one of the old fashioned telephone kiosks (I don't think it would be possible in one of the new ones). Could we get into trouble doing this?

Only if someone who sees you complains and you get caught. And then, even if the court shows you mercy, the resulting publicity could be embarrassing. You could, I suppose, always claim that you were both suffering from hypothermia – and were trying to warm one another up.

You weren't in Rome on February 17th were you? Do you have a little butterfly tattoo on your left breast? If that was you I've got some wonderful photos you might like.

●●●

Teenage Crush

I am 42 years and quite happily married. The family next door have a 16 year old girl who seems to have developed a crush on me. Whenever I see her she flirts with me outrageously. At first I was embarrassed but I confess that I have recently found her attention flattering and exciting. My wife was out of the house yesterday and she came round to ask me to help her with some homework. She was wearing a very short skirt, a thin T shirt and little or nothing else. While we were sitting together on the sofa she got closer and closer to me. She was pretending to take an interest in what I was writing in her notebook but she obviously wanted me to kiss her and in the end I did. I'm absolutely certain that if I had wanted her to go further she would have been quite happy to do anything I wanted her to do. I don't know what the hell to do now. I would dearly love to take her to bed but I have a suspicion that I'm playing with dynamite.

Whoa! Down boy! I prescribe cold showers three times a day. Next time you see this girl and feel a stirring in your groin try to believe that you've got a pressure sensitive anti-personnel mine strapped into your underpants.

You aren't playing with dynamite. People play with dynamite and live. You are blindfold, naked and drunk and you are juggling with half a dozen petrol driven chain saws while walking a cheese wire above a 5,000 foot drop into a shark infested lake.

Of course, you'll have fun. Wonderful gravity resistant breasts. Eager, adoring eyes. Firm skin like soft velvet. Magic, stolen, secret moments of loving. And then she will fall in love with a spotty 17 year old and tell her Dad about you. Blame. Wagging fingers. Cruel accusations. Little miss sixteen will wreck your marriage, ruin your reputation and suck you dry.

I suggest that you smile sweetly when you see her but make sure you're never alone with her again.

•••

Torrid Affair

My husband recently found out that I had had a brief, casual and rather torrid affair with a man I met through my work. It wasn't a love affair – it was just sex. My husband made me tell him all about it. He wanted to know what we'd done together, how often we'd done it, where we'd done it and so on. He wasn't satisfied until I'd told him everything in great detail. He even made me describe the other man's penis. Afterwards my husband made love to me quite fiercely. It was the best sex we've ever had. He didn't say anything but I got the impression that my confessions had excited him. And I suspect he would like me to do it again with someone else. Could I be right?

You could be. Some men do get excited by the knowledge that their partners have been making love to other men. But I strongly suggest that before you follow your hunch you talk about this. Even if he gets turned on by your infidelity your husband will probably want to lay down some ground rules. Safe sex at all times. Nothing indiscreet. No anal sex. That sort of thing.

•••

Not Sure What To Do

I would like to try oral sex but I am not sure what to do. I am rather shy and a little bit worried about putting my foot in it.

Don't worry too much about putting your foot in it. This is unlikely unless you are a contortionist with uncontrollable muscle spasms.

●●●

Glue Like

I've been dating my current boyfriend for 4 weeks. He enjoys me masturbating him but his semen is very thick and glue like. It doesn't spurt out but just sort of sits on the end of his penis. All my previous boyfriends made quite a mess when ejaculating and this turned me on. Is there anything wrong with my boyfriend? Will he be infertile? Is there anything we can do to make his semen more runny?

Semen is usually sticky and creamy. It is thick immediately after ejaculation, then becomes more liquid and eventually dries after exposure to the air. (The white stain can usually be removed with a stiff brush and a weak solution of sodium bicarbonate. Semen stains are fluorescent under ultraviolet light, by the way). The colour varies but is normally white, grey or yellow. The distance a man fires his semen varies and the world record is eight feet eight inches. This doesn't have much influence over his chances of becoming a father (though the ancient Hebrews used to believe that sperm which didn't come out forcefully wasn't fertile) since sperm can swim and as long as they're deposited in the right general area they can make their way up into the womb by themselves. There are several possible reasons for a change in a man's ejaculatory pattern. These include increasing age, diabetes, back injury and prostate trouble. Some drugs are known to have an effect on the amount of semen and the distance it travels after leaving the penis. Your boyfriend should have a word with his doctor.

●●●

Unusual Fantasy

While having sex with my husband I don't fantasise about other men like I know a lot of women do. Instead I fantasise about my husband having sex with other women. This really turns me on although I know I wouldn't want him to do it in real life. He knows about my fantasy and tells me what he would like to do them. Sometimes we fantasise together about real women we both know. Are there any other women like me?

Yes. An entirely unreliable survey conducted recently showed that 72% of women with breasts of A cup size or larger regularly fantasised about their husbands making love to other women. There are absolutely no rules in fantasy land. No rights, no wrongs and no need ever to feel guilty. Fantasising is healthy and much cheaper, less troublesome and more effective than psychoanalysis. You can get rid of hidden fears, hopes, and guilts through sexual fantasies. You can exorcise unidentified ghosts and enjoy yourself without worrying about boundaries or what the neighbours will say. It is particularly wonderful that you and your husband can share a fantasy world. And it must be quite fun to be able to listen to your husband's wild and unbridled fantasies about that pompous woman in tweeds who always talks as though she's got her mouth full and walks as though she's got a prize winning courgette stuck up her bum.

●●●

Things Got Out Of Hand

During a recent holiday in Ilfracombe my husband and I were sitting cuddling on a bench overlooking the sea when things got rather out of hand. We both decided we wanted more than just a cuddle but our hotel was about two miles away and we didn't want to wait that long. We ended up making love on the bench with me sitting on his lap with my knickers in my handbag and my dress pulled up to my thighs. It was the best sex either of us have ever had. What made it exciting was that several people walked by as we doing it and no one had any idea what we were doing. Afterwards we did it outdoors on several other occasions. Is there any law about having sex in public places? Could we get into trouble if we got caught?

I'm sure you could get into trouble if you got caught for outdoor sex is bound to be a breach of some penile code. I haven't the foggiest what they'd do you for. Behaviour likely to lead to a breach of the peace? Behaviour likely to make puritanical Presbyterians feel jealous and extremely upset? Behaviour likely to make other people realise what they've been missing for the past 96 years? Behaviour likely to result in a large crowd of people gathering and yelling bawdy encouragement? One thing is for sure: if you're spotted enjoying yourselves in public there is bound to be a law against it and the end result will be that having been screwed by your husband you'll get screwed by the system. My carefully thought out advice is that you should try not to get caught. And if you do get spotted then have a good excuse ready. Alternatively, I know of one couple who escaped prosecution at a Northern seaside resort by arguing that they were both just trying to keep warm. With the right excuse you'd probably get a discharge which is, I suppose, where your troubles started.

●●

Being Honest

While we were in bed my boyfriend asked me if his whatsit was as big as all the other whatsits I'd had. I always believe in being honest so I told him it wasn't. In fact I told him that it was the smallest I'd ever seen. When he asked me if I preferred big ones I said I did. He said that it wasn't the size but what you did with it that really counted but I said that was nonsense. He then went all quiet and disappeared. Half an hour later I found him in the bathroom crying.

I'm surprised he hadn't slit his wrists. How would you feel if he had told you that your breasts were too small and that you had a harbour big enough for the QE II to be moored? Men worry about these things and like women to be tactful. In this instance tact usually involves a certain amount of dishonesty. If you love him would it have really hurt you to lie a little?

•••

I Sleep With The Landlord

When my husband lost his job last year we found ourselves in a lot of debt. When we fell behind with the rent the landlord offered to let us live rent free if I slept with him two evenings every week. I thought my husband would object but he was quite happy – especially since the landlord gives him a few quid to go to the pub when its his nights to 'collect'. Last week the washing machine broke down and my husband spoke to the engineer who said he would fix it if I had sex with him. I quite fancy him – he is only in his 20s and quite good looking – but I can't help wondering where all this is leading.

A quick telephone poll of a representative sample of voters shows that everyone who studies this abbreviated version of your life story is convinced that you are heading for a career for which the accepted uniform consists of red, five inch heels, black underwear, a microskirt and a see through blouse and where the acknowledged occupational hazards include gluteal friction burns, sucker's lips and humper's pubic rub.

Yesterday it was the rent and today it is the washing machine. What is it going to be tomorrow? Are you really so naive that you can't see where all this is taking you? Or do you have your head buried so far in the sand that you can't see what is happening at the other end of your body?

Whoring is a perfectly sound and morally unimpeachable way to earn a living. There are hazards (some – but not all – of which can be minimised by the use of condoms) but if you're going to pay your way with squidgy currency you should start by being honest with yourself.

●●●

A Lot Of Erections

I am 17. My problem is that I get a lot of erections. My penis often stays that way for ages. I have tried re-straining it with sticky tape. I do not approve of masturbation.

Put the sticky tape away. As long as your erections come and go in the regular way your problem is simply a normal consequence of being seventeen. Teenage erections may come for no apparent reason: circulating hormones and external, erotic stimulations can all be to blame. Within a few years you will look back upon these bountiful days of plenty with a green eyed memory. If your bulge embarrasses you then wear baggy clothing or long jumpers to maintain your secret.

●●●

Loving Son

I am 37 and have a 22 year old son. My husband left me when my baby was born. I am financially comfortable and my son has a good job. He is tall, fit and strong and plays football and cricket. My problem is that he has always slept with me and since he was 16 we have had a sexual relationship. There are times when I have an almost overwhelming urge to have his baby. He is quite willing and keen to have a baby with me. Would you please tell me what my prospects are of having a normal child. We are both in good health. I know that if I wait much longer I will be too old.

I don't think you should have a baby by your son. Every one of us carries at least one gene for a harmful disorder – and probably at least two for conditions that would result in a dead baby. Since you and your son may carry the same genes the risk of you giving birth to a dead or seriously deformed or mentally retarded baby is around 1 in 2. Those are terrible odds.

• •

Noise In The Bedroom

I am 33 years old and have been married for ten years. For some time I have not been very interested in sex. When my husband approaches me I make excuses to avoid it.

I recently came home early from work. I went into the house quietly as my husband was in bed after his night shift. As I went upstairs I heard a noise in the bedroom. I peered in through the crack between the door and the door frame and saw my husband lying naked on the bed wearing a pair of my stockings and playing with himself.

91

I quickly and quietly went back downstairs and opened and closed the door as though I had just come in. My husband got up and acted as if nothing had happened.

That night, when he had gone to work I lay in bed thinking of what had I had seen. I have to admit that I was very excited by it. The thought of him in my underwear excited me a lot. I masturbated to a climax very quickly.

Do you think I should tell him what I saw as I think it would help our sex life. The thought of making love to him dressed up is a real turn on for me.

I don't think you should tell him that you saw him. He might be embarrassed. But why don't you bring the subject up as though it was your idea? You could, for example, say that you'd seen a letter or an article about men who wear women's clothing and you had wondered whether he had ever fancied the idea. You can hint that you had found the thought a turn on. The moment has to be right, of course. Lying in bed together is a good moment. Sitting round the table entertaining the in laws is not a good moment.

●●●

Can't Get Enough

My husband can't get enough sex. He says he gets pain in his testicles if he doesn't have sex at least two or three times a day. I am exhausted. We do it every morning and every evening – sometimes for two hours at a time – and my vagina is constantly sore. Once he made love to me six times in a row with hardly a break in between. Do you think he should see his doctor? I know this sounds odd but it has got to the stage where I would be happy if he'd find a mistress to take a bit of the pressure off me.

Yes, your husband should see his doctor. There could be a physical (and hopefully a soluble) explanation for his exhausting sexual appetite. Meanwhile, rather than finding him a mistress why not give your vagina a rest by providing him with manual relief.

•••

At The Christmas Party

My boss kissed me at our Christmas Party. While he was kissing me he fondled my breasts through my dress. I haven't been able to think about anything else since then. I think I have fallen in love with him. I've worked under him for three years but had never before realised that he felt this way about me. How do I tell him the way I feel?

I think I must have missed something. Maybe a page of your letter got lost in the post. I hate to be boringly realistic but don't you think it could be possible that you may be reading just a little too much into your boss's behaviour? Isn't it possible that you were simply groped by a man who was a little overfull of Christmas spirit? I think you should wait until you get your breasts fondled a second time before you start sending out the wedding invitations.

•••

A Philanderer

My husband is a philanderer.

Don't worry. Lots of men collect stamps.

•••

A Bad Lover

My boyfriend isn't very good at sex. He blames the size and shape of his penis but I've had boyfriends with smaller penises who were better lovers.

A bad lover always blames his tool.

●●

*For a full catalogue of Vernon Coleman's books
please write to*

*Publishing House,
Trinity Place, Barnstaple,
Devon
EX32 9HJ
England*

*Telephone: 01271 328892
Fax: 01271 328768*

*Or visit our web site
www.vernoncoleman.com*